M000033102

"THE ENERGY OF A
SINGLE THOUGHT
MAY DETERMINE
   THE MOTION OF A
UNIVERSE."
   - NIKOLA TESLA

ABOUT NEXT THIRTY PRESS

At Next Thirty Press, we want to publish the type of knowledge and ideas that can fuel the next thirty years of progress for mankind, that could make the world a closer and better place, and can inspire its future leaders.

ABOUT NEXT THIRTY IDEABOOKS

The Next30 Ideabook is our reimagining of the business book. Long enough to introduce strong, new ideas, but short enough to be read quickly by busy people. Not too dry, and not without insight. Offered in a package that is easy to carry and a casually inspiring read.

INNOVATION THINKING METHODS

FOR THE MODERN ENTREPRENEUR

DISCIPLINES OF THOUGHT THAT CAN HELP YOU RETHINK INDUSTRIES AND UNLOCK 10X BETTER SOLUTIONS

BY: OSAMA A. HASHMI

Copyright © 2016 by Osama A. Hashmi

All rights reserved. This book or any portion thereof may not be reproduced or used in any manner whatsoever without the express written permission of the publisher, except for the use of brief quotations in a book review and certain other noncommercial uses permitted by copyright law. For permission requests, write to the publisher at the address below, or via email at permissions@next30. press

Next Thirty Press
9450 SW Gemini Drive #87366
Beaverton, OR 97008
www.next30.press

Library of Congress Control Number: 2016903457

Publisher's Cataloging-in-Publication data

Names: Hashmi, Osama A., author.
Title: Innovation thinking methods for the modern entrepreneur : disciplines of thought that can help you rethink industries and unlock 10x better solutions / Osama A. Hashmi.
Description: First edition | Beaverton [Oregon]: Next Thirty Press, 2016.
Identifiers: ISBN 978-0-9973587-2-8 (Hardcover) | ISBN 978-0-9973587-1-1 (pbk.) |ISBN 978-0-9973587-0-4 (ebook) | LCCN 2016903457.
Subjects: LCSH Entrepreneurship. | Success in business. | Business enterprises. | New business enterprises. | Problem solving. | Decision making. | Creative ability in business. | BISAC BUSINESS & ECONOMICS / Entrepreneurship | BUSINESS & ECONOMICS / Business Writing | BUSINESS & ECONOMICS / Decision-Making & Problem Solving.
Classification: LCC HD62.5 .H37395 2016 | DDC 658.041--dc23

PRINTED IN THE UNITED STATES OF AMERICA

1000 cranes for Japan Illustration on Cover by Jden Redden. Coffee cups illustration by Freepik.com. Escape Velocity liftoff Illustration by Andrew Mitchell.

Additional Credits Appear on Page 129, which constitutes a continuation of this copyright page.

First Edition
14 13 12 11 10 / 5 4 3 2 1

CONTENTS

For my two grandmothers - Ami Ji and Bari Ami - who both passed away in 2015 within a few months of one another, during the short course of writing this book.

I will always remember every smile, piece of advice, and encouragement from you, and will continue to try and improve myself based on the inspiration from your lives, and will work to be a part of the potential for positive change you saw in the world.

AUTHOR'S PREFACE: COFFEE SESSIONS AND THOUGHT EXPERIMENTS (AND NOT PREPARING FOR THE MACHINES TO TAKE OVER)

If you've just discovered my writing: I think of business writing as you and I having coffee and exploring meaningful questions together - a "Coffee Session". Nice to meet you. Let's settle in by that fireplace over there.

Innovation-thinking is something I've been meaning to write about for some time. I used to write and speak regularly about these topics some years ago as part of running larger entrepreneurship support initiatives, but since then I went on to focus on my companies and haven't been able to write much.

In recent years, startups and the startup support eco-system seems to be trending towards the "safe and steady", and I think it's time to start a conversation on rebuilding an orientation towards big thinking. What you'll find here is part of a framework of thought I've used to help shift the mind towards innovative solutions. It draws from my experiences coaching, mentoring, consulting companies on tech product strategy, and working with and learning from brilliant innovative minds, and building teams with strong innovation cultures who end up solving very hard problems and creating brilliant products, that I'm proud to have been able to do.

Thing is, as a writer, if there are things you've been meaning to say for a long time, it's too tempting to end up making a book that talks about all aspects of something... a 300+ page, overwhelming, self-contained reference guide, as if it was written for a future where the machines take over and eliminate access to all digital knowledge.

It's tempting to end up with a book where the words are all prophetic-sounding, as if etched in marble... to be a beacon for archaeologists of the future to unearth from the dark, charred remains of post-A.I. civilization.

(As you can tell, my writing tends to be a bit cheeky from time to time - it's just to bring some levity to serious topics, I don't mean anything by it.)

Those types of books can be hard to commit the time to read. Instead, I wanted this book to be a quick read for busy people, with what I call a high DGP index ("Density of Goodness per Page").

That's why Next30's ideabook format felt perfect for this - something in between blogs and traditional business books.

Here, if there's a concept that has enough material already available online, I won't spend too much time explaining it, trusting you to know best if you want to just look it up as you read along. That way, hopefully the book will only focus on meaningful or additive stuff.

I'll keep personal anecdotes to a minimum, and try to maximize substance. And I'll try to avoid all startup-speak (seriously, if you hear me do startup-speak, take my coffee away. Trust me, that *hurts*).

And the teaching method here will be more interactive. I won't be going through detailed examples or case-studies from my work. Something that worked for me or my clients, for those specific situations may not apply to you. Instead, I'll aim to teach through thought-experiments. That way, you can take the situation you're in, the life and opportunities you're seeing around you, and after each chapter, try and apply that thinking method to discover specific solutions.

What's best: This short format is more efficient overall both for you as a reader, and for me as a writer.

Alright, everything sorted?

Then let's dive into some deep, deep coffee.

[Long-time readers: That last sentence was for you]

WHO IS THIS BOOK FOR?

While this book was written primarily for entrepreneurs or innovation-focused product teams, or people broadly in the tech industry, I've heard from readers of early drafts of this book that the information within is also useful for people in other fields.

I think strong innovation is going to be the need of this decade regardless of who you are and what you're doing professionally - whether you're building a startup, part of an innovation team in a larger company, part of a mission-driven non-profit, or part of any project that wants to do more ambitious things.

So if you are someone wanting to kickstart ambitious thinking inside of your work-life, this book may be for you.

Okay, coffee's brewed now, so let's go.

1 SO, WHAT IS INNOVATION-THINKING?

I'D LIKE THE WORLD to start thinking more innovatively. It's a simple request, really.

A lot of my professional life has been related to building tech product companies; enabling, mentoring and helping entrepreneurs; helping tech companies with product innovation and strategy; or overseeing product launches (the Author Blurb at the end covers it more specifically). I've seen hundreds of product launches and spoken to many more startups or entrepreneurs.

So my request is born out of seeing too many products of the same type being made again and again in recent years, most often based on principles of incremental derivative improvement; "improving on competitors"; data-driven decisions; micro-optimizing conversion rates; and more. "Lean Methods" seem to have become the norm (by the way, by "Lean Methods" I'm including all the popular lean methods out there now: lean startup, lean canvas, lean marketing, lean customer development, lean latte-making, what have you).

There's nothing inherently wrong with Lean Methods - I talk about them more at the end of the book - but they seem to make highly talented startup teams do mediocre things.

I mean, we have these people in society who are unusually wired to be able to handle massive risk, hold the ability to tolerate insane work-hours, and the capacity for thought that can invent things from nothing. But more and more, I'm seeing brilliant people use that energy for creation to make things like photo apps for weddings; appointment setting systems for dogs and pet-doctors; yet-another invoicing software; yet-another pizza-ordering solution; and other things not suited for that type of thinking capacity and talent.

Rather than aiming to hit things out of the park with each step, with an obsessive "nothing to lose" hunger, more and more I'm finding entrepreneurs becoming hesitant to be bold-thinkers until the data supports it; ignoring domain insight or tacit knowledge for the shallow uncertainty of pivots; and obsessing more about A/B tests rather than obsessing about adding delight in their products.

Innovation seems to have been left too long to the forces that champion complacency of thought... and it may be turning our brightest emerging minds into zombies.

This actually has real consequence. With an abundance of "incrementally better but otherwise the same" products in the market, the attention that customers are paying to any of them is dropping rapidly. Ironically then, if the support ecosystem for entrepreneurs focuses only on reducing risk of failure for startups (with an experiments-driven approach with minimal outlay), that would increase the risk of obscurity for those startups, which greatly increases their risk of failure. (I'll expand on this in an addendum at the end of the book).

I guess I've had too much coffee, but looking over the past 150 years - and even presently - I've found that the companies that see massive growth, that make a difference in their industries and in the lives of others, and create large exits and returns for all shareholders... they just do things differently.

They are companies that seek to create new demand, or expand markets, rather than fight over a shrinking percentage of existing markets.

They make products worth noticing, and worth talking about, and worth evangelizing, the ones that inspire change in the minds of people, even those elusive people who are classically "hard to change the habits of". They understand attention-economics - that more of the same but 10% better isn't going to get attention.

They look at products not just as things that can make some quick money today, for today's demand - products that just barely implement the minimum that customers want. They see products as something that inspire and surprise beyond what customers thought was possible, giving them new abilities, by getting a thousand details just right.

These companies don't compete with competitors, they jump curves, making all competitors suddenly irrelevant and drastically inferior.

Most importantly, they find a 10x better future worth striving for, that ignites a fire in the hearts of founders and their startup teams that is worth pursuing, that makes them want to quit and jump in head-first, that carries them through all the darkness and brutal hardship of startup life when there's nary any coffee in sight (the horror), through all the cynicism and forces that try to stop change or innovation, through all the hesitations from customers, through all the fears of risk-averse investors or supporters. It is the thing those teams are happy to do even 10 years after founding the company.

But... how do we find that 10x better thing? That idea worth executing?

And how do we find the thousands of new ideas that form the heart of great execution?

We do it by changing the lens through which we view the world. By discarding a lens of hypothesis-until-data-verified, of "improving on competitors", of incremental solutions.

We do it through a lens that I'm calling "innovation-thinking" - an orientation towards wanting to find meaningful, substantial solutions that can bring about positive change in the world, as a problem solving device at every stage of a company, through the application of specific disciplines of thought.

It has taken me some time to realize and accept that innovation-thinking is its own encompassing framework, is separate from "design-thinking", and is perhaps not commonly practiced. I've been lucky that all the teams in my companies have made it a part of their norm for work. We just thought of it as our internal process of creativity or strategic thinking, and assumed everyone else does it too.

"Design-Thinking" is a similar framework of thought, but it is focused on better understanding customer needs to help polish out products and add more empathy into them.

But "Innovation-Thinking" is an orientation of thought with a different goal: To help create radically better ("10x better") solutions, for every business function (e.g. pricing, sales, marketing etc.), not just in product definition or vision-setting, using specific innovation-thinking methods when brainstorming to shift the mind towards big ideas.

Some of these methods are hundreds of years old, and come from philosophy. Some are things analysts, futurists or economists tend to develop as skills to frame the future. Some of these are just unblockers - to help if our ideas are becoming too derivative. Some of these are inspired by books or talks or movies or culture. Some may be new.

In this book, I'm presenting just a few of the innovation-thinking methods I've discovered and practiced over my career. We use these daily at my two companies CDF Software (a stealth software product company), and Mocha7 (a strategy consulting firm). We use them with clients, and I've used them when mentoring entrepreneurs, and even when I worked as an analyst or management consultant. They've always helped in creating great results.

I'm presenting them here so that companies like us - who say "we're not a lean startup company, we do innovation-thinking" - can more easily find people who we'd like to work with, and find support from people who really get what we are aiming to do.

But that's just part of a larger discussion on what an "Innovation-thinking company" could look like, that I touch on in an addendum at the end.

First, you've got to get familiar with some of these methods.

Let's get into them.

2 METHOD ZERO: TALK AND BEHAVE LIKE A HUMAN

I'VE MADE A COMMITMENT in my life to always try and speak like a human in business contexts. To be a bit cheeky, and light-hearted (to forever hold and cherish coffee, in warmth and in re-heats...).

My favorite was pitching one of my companies to a room full of investors, hedge-fund managers, bankers, and CEOs (20 people in all) at a very exclusive high-stakes event, by talking for two minutes about Mater from the Pixar movie Cars.

There's an important business reason for this commitment to being human.

Too often we tend to focus on communicating that we

are taking business matters seriously. So, we do this by behaving very seriously about business matters. We start speaking grimly and with heavy-weighted profound-sounding words. We start to think that solutions can only come from the framework of business language and concepts that are well-known.

I think in doing so we lock ourselves out from influences that can often lead to more creative ways of looking at business problems, leading to more interesting solutions.

Speaking like a human doesn't have to be the same as being non-serious about the work being done, or problems being solved, or things we're aiming to accomplish.

We certainly want to be razor focused on actual useful business results, but in focusing on being human along the way to those results, it helps us take inspiration and influence from things outside of that business context, from culture, from sociology, from nature, from science-fiction, etc.

That's all that idea-creation and innovation needs sometimes. To figure out how to push the mind to shift its perspective and look at things slightly differently. Seeing through that different lens, new discoveries and insights are often easily found.

That's what this book is about - "disciplines of thought" to get our mind to shift just slightly enough to be more innovative, whatever it takes.

So you might find some of these techniques to be a bit simple or silly on paper. They're trying to help you make $MM decisions by referencing movies, or doing weird thought-experiments.

But that focus on thinking and talking like humans - using *very simple* concepts and *minimum shift* in effort to create *maximum improvement in results* - is precisely what makes these techniques work, by helping to unblock and kickstart our mind into forward-thinking again, even if it takes a QUOTE FROM COMMANDER ADAMA[1] to do so.

This is something I've learned from observing the best communicators in the world. The only reason I still know anything about Computer Architecture is because of Dr. Yale Patt, who in his courses is never afraid of speaking like it was a Saturday morning cartoon if it helps get a point across.

Seth Godin isn't afraid of making people laugh through simple examples, or by showing off his socks to get a point across, and that makes his lessons incredibly inspiring.

So keep that focus in mind when you read ahead.

Oh and that presentation about Mater from Pixar's Cars? That's a presentation technique: "Reframe and refocus", which helps to clear pre-built expectations from the minds of an audience and thus improve their attention on the actual thing

---

1   "Sometimes you have to roll a hard six", Feld.com. Accessed Jan 3, 2016. http://www.feld.com/archives/2013/12/sometimes-you-have-to-roll-a-hard-six.html

you've come to say. It was one of the most successful pitches we've done.

One last thing about being human. I've found being human also opens up the chance to hear the most interesting perspectives or ideas from other people, that can constantly help teach new things and new ways of looking at the world. It allows for that honesty about things we know and things we don't know, about knowledge or experience others can offer that help to fill in those gaps.

3 FIRST PRINCIPLES THINKING

THIS METHOD IS CLEARLY the first thing we should talk about, since it's been front-of-mind in many a recent debate on innovation-thinking.

In the spirit of this short-book format, however, I won't linger on this method too long since this is also one you have probably heard or read about already, and there is a lot of material about it available online for further study.

First Principles Thinking is an innovation-thinking method popularized recently after it was explained by Elon Musk in an INTERVIEW WITH KEVIN ROSE[1], but its roots in philosophy and

---

1   "The First Principles Method Explained by Elon Musk" Youtube.com. Accessed Jan 6, 2016. https://www.youtube.com/watch?v=NV3sBlRgzTI

logic trace also to ARISTOTLE[2], Descartes and others. Here's a direct quote on how Elon explained it:

> *"I think it's important to reason from first principles rather than by analogy. The normal way we conduct our lives is we reason by analogy. [With analogy] we are doing this because it's like something else that was done, or it is like what other people are doing. [With first principles] you boil things down to the most fundamental truths...and then reason up from there."*

The idea is to seek fundamental truths that will always remain true, after you remove all the things that don't necessarily have to remain true. Descartes, for example, used CARTESIAN DOUBT[3] to doubt everything he could possibly doubt, until something remained in the logic that couldn't be doubted.

In other fields, you can apply it as removing everything that is just "the current way something works" until you get to the "always true" things - things that always must be a part of something. Then, when you are unable to see something breaking down further - something that always must happen, or always must be the way it is - you can build up to the fastest and most efficient way of getting that base thing done.

As an example, what is the fundamental truth of what defines a "car"? A car doesn't actually *need* to have any part of the way cars are designed today. It doesn't need a combustible fuel engine, it doesn't need for you to manually drive it, it doesn't need a suspension or even tires. The most basic form of a "car" is just some sort of a container which you enter, and it travels horizontally around on roads following road regulations, and gets you from A to B, after which you get out of it.

Given that base form, you can now rethink and re-imagine cars to be anything, and rethink their manufacturing, assembly, seat design etc accordingly. Chances are, whatever you do end up creating will be considered substantially "innovative", or will at least give you the opportunity to massively reduce its build-costs.

A corollary way of applying first-principles is in project planning, which goes something like: "Once we eliminate and fix everything that could possibly go wrong in our plan, and eliminate any assumptions we've taken, whatever remains must be a plan we can bank on."

Anyway, as I said, if you're interested in further study on this method there is a lot of material online you can find. So, for now, we will move onward.

4 CHANGE THE STARTUP PITCH FORMULA FOR DISRUPTIVE THINKING

SOMETIMES, INNOVATION-THINKING COMES FROM considering how to get investors excited about your company. (Note: this isn't quite advice for how to do fundraising, but rather this is another thing to help you discover more innovative solutions.)

You may have heard a vague statement a number of times: that investors are looking for a "huge market" and a "product with huge future potential." More specifically you may have heard "Investors want to hear a clear story about how this company can go after massive market potential and

14

disrupt / dominate that space / make a big impact."

Now, separately to this, common startup pitch advice encourages companies to design a pitch / story of their company that describes three things separately:

- What is a problem a typical user has in his or her life

- What does the product do to solve this problem

- How many of those users are there (hence big market)

The problem is, done literally (where each thing is treated as a separate concern), this isn't really a very compelling story. More importantly for us right now, it doesn't really serve well as a "method for thinking innovatively", as working through a pitch like that can just as easily lead only to the most derivative or mundane of improvements in the smallest of niches.

Let's take a look at an alternative.

I've found a good many times that filling the blanks on the sentence below actually helps to not only build that compelling story, but also helps to find the type of innovation that can have a significant impact with a great opportunity.

> "Currently the cost economies of products
> in _____ market are too high to (either go after this significant percentage of

> market that is untapped, OR out-compete
> the incumbents at this game.) *However,*
> *if* (this specific technology) *is made by*
> *our team, we believe we can bring down*
> *the economies to this point where we* CAN
> *serve / disrupt that market significantly."*

That sounds convoluted - so let's look at some examples to understand this better.

We can start by looking at some of the early interviews of SpaceX and how the company pitched its investment potential (they have PUBLISHED THE PITCH ON THEIR WEBSITE[1]). I'm paraphrasing / rewriting it to fit our key sentence.

> *(paraphrased) "The economies of space*
> *travel currently keeps it unfeasible for*
> *many corporations and businesses to*
> *consider it part of their strategy, and the*
> *key problem is that rockets aren't reusable.*
> *If we can make basic rockets reusable as*
> *takeoff + landing systems, we'd be able to*
> *see massive improvements in the costs per*
> *trip, as the cost of manufacturing could*
> *be spread over life-time uses. This could*
> *reduce per-trip cost of space-travel by*

---

1   "Reusability: The Key to Making Human Life Multi-Planetary", SpaceX. com, June 10, 2015. http://www.spacex.com/news/2013/03/31/reusability-key-making-human-life-multi-planetary

> *factors of 10,000x or more, bringing the*
> *economies into the range where things like*
> *space tourism, mining, logistics and a lot*
> *more could be viable, feasible and profitable*
> *for many corporate businesses. And that*
> *would have a significant impact."*

A friend once was running a social entrepreneurship venture I was particularly fond of. Her pitch / story was essentially the same:

> *(paraphrased) "Currently mineral water*
> *companies only serve the upper 50% of*
> *the market, leaving 50% of the market*
> *unserved. This is because the cost of pro-*
> *ducing and shipping mineral water bottles*
> *to the lower-end isn't profitable. BUT if*
> *we could make [their key technology] we*
> *can not only massively reduce manufac-*
> *turing costs because of not having to need*
> *large production facilities, but also sim-*
> *plify logistics, thus driving the economics*
> *of per-unit manufacturing so much lower*
> *than before, that it then becomes viable /*
> *feasible / profitable to serve the lower 50%*
> *market. The company that does this could*
> *be as big as Nestle or other giants in this*
> *space because of the size of the unserved*

market, and that can be a big thing."

Another friend built and is actively involved in a large non-profit hospital for the rural poor, that is almost entirely based on tele-medicine. His pitch could be summarized in a similar way (you can support the non-profit HERE[2] if you'd like).

> *The typical cost of healthcare is prohib-*
> *itively expensive for people of [this rural*
> *area] given the poverty in the region. The*
> *key problem is staffing a hospital that is so*
> *remote with doctors, and the costs / logis-*
> *tics overhead of having them make the trip.*
> *However, with [the technology of tele-med-*
> *icine] we separate the location from the*
> *doctor. Since doctors could then practically*
> *be anywhere in the world, and since they*
> *wouldn't have to deal with a fixed schedule*
> *or logistics, we can see massive economies*
> *in the cost of delivery of healthcare, to a*
> *point closer to what those communities can*
> *afford. That makes a big impact.*

These all sound fairly compelling, right?

This same reason can be applied to most companies that

---

2   "Make Healthcare accessible to poor via Technology", Globalgiving. org, Accessed Jan 4, 2016. https://www.globalgiving.org/projects/health-care-through-mobile-technology/

tend to garner massive excitement about their potential. Electric cars for example - at a certain scale - can become cheaper to manufacture compared to their petrol equivalents.

Companies like AirBnB and Lyft massively reduce economies of operating a hotel / cab-company business [by outsourcing asset and inventory management], which is precisely why those respective industries are worried about them.

The company Bank Simple pitches the same thing for reducing the operating costs of banks, because of branch-less banking.

The smartphone movement, by the way, has enabled a LOT of this type of innovation thinking. Everything that was economically unfeasible because it required dedicated hardware to deliver as a solution, now could be done with software and some dongles, greatly improving the cost economies. E.g. Square's big opportunity has been getting the everyday folks - the yoga instructors, individuals, freelancers, to all be able to carry a credit card machine along with them wherever they go. This was an untapped market, otherwise inaccessible due to the older bank card machines and contracts etc.

Yet... consider the alternative pitch. Maybe the type of pitch someone you know made, or was thinking of making. Something like this:

> Hi - I'm so-and-so. We are changing the
> way people make invoices. The problem

is currently invoices take all of 4 clicks to make. But with our mobile app, its a simple tap and flick gesture and its off. Our app is #5 is the app store for our category and growing at XYZ% weekly.

Hi, I'm so-and-so, and we're rethinking the way people go to the movies. Currently going to the movies is such a complex process with having to make plans with friends and looking up movie times - but our solution is the app picks the movie and the friends to watch with automatically - you're just expected to show up and have fun, whatever the combination. It's in private alpha and we're crushing it.

These don't really seem as exciting or focused on a large opportunity for disruption, right?

The thought process here is that great companies use technology to break open a key barrier to either expanding the market or out-pricing / out-executing existing market players in a *significant* way - in a way that affects *everybody* in that market.

What's more, that new place you end up in - the part of the market that no one is able to get to - is a great place.

There's no competition, the entire field is open to you and you alone.

That's the type of story that appeals to investors the most - a huge untapped area, enabled only by your technology, that leads to a place with no competition.

The other type of pitch, the "we're the so-and-so for so-and-so and solving a niche problem" tends to fall into a separate bucket. That's what you may call the "Okay, I guess we'll support them a bit and see where it goes" bucket.

In any case, it should help better frame your conversations on how to disrupt and challenge market incumbents.

5 THE ONE-SENTENCE METHOD

PEOPLE OVER TIME WILL forget a lot of details of what they learn about a subject, but will always retain one core essence of that subject.

My micro-economics professor in college was the first to explain that to me, arguing, "If there is one thing you should remember when you think micro-economics, it's the words 'supply' and 'demand'."

I found that curious, and started applying it to other functional roles of a company too. I've found since then that just distilling fields of work down to a single core essence greatly helps to innovate and keep ahead of the curve in them.

Lets take Marketing.

I define marketing as: "How do you walk into a jubilant party where everyone is talking to one another, and what do you say or do that makes them stop talking, turn around and look at you?"

In a shorter sentence: "Marketing = What do I say or do that is worth paying attention to?"

If you just keep fixed on that one goal, and figure out the rest along the way, that will give you a better chance of innovating and trying out new things (and if the stars align, we'll finally have people move away from putting junk content out there just because they read somewhere that that's what you're meant to do - oh please can those stars just align already?)

I've been on the board of Mocha7 since founding it in 2009. Mocha7's team does consulting on innovation, product and marketing strategy. We founded that company partly because we'd happened to discover some approaches that seemed to be very effective at attention-getting at the time - these today are generally called Advocacy Marketing and Community-Building.

Since then we've discovered how rapidly the marketing industry reinvents itself. These days, the industry keeps changing every four months or so on the clock, reinventing all its secrets, methods, techniques and channels, as newer and newer platforms and mediums emerge. In fact, these days the top-end firms aren't even waiting for new platforms to emerge, as they are just building up teams of engineers to help them build new platforms as needed.

For example, looking just at Content Marketing, about 4-5 years ago attention was driven primarily through blogs and text-based content discovery. Then attention moved to visual content like Infographics or image lists, then hopped through video and around many other things; nowadays attention lies in interactive, playable content; in consumable content that fills space between things in life (e.g. podcasts) and long-form content like books. And it will change again in about three months.

So the team at Mocha7 uses this one-sentence approach to keep up and stay competitive, even against bigger and more established firms. Every four months or so, they huddle together to ask that question again: "If Marketing is just getting people's attention, how do we do it now given these new mediums and tools?" and create some new tactics or approaches to try out.

Side-note: That's also why I've been interested in this "short-book" format - to rapidly publish things so they are still fresh in their relevance. Most books that go through a traditional book-publishing process (10-20 months) are heavily out of date in insights by the time they come to market (but more on that some other time in some other book).

Going back to that party example though, it's fun to define Sales as well.

In that party, Sales would be looking at all the people who are (now) looking at you, noticing who has their eyebrows arched upwards, and going and shaking their hands.

That boils down to "how do I effectively filter to try and understand who is most interested, and prioritize my time hearing about their interests and needs", which would help in more interesting approaches on how to do that filter, how to spend more time with them, how to be more wary of their interests, etc.

These core essences of professions are timeless, somewhat like the first-principles of these fields, and learning the discipline to get back to it - to create a blank slate every once in a while and relearning and rediscovering everything about that field from that essence keeps you on the edge.

6 THE FUTURE HISTORY APPROACH

AMAZON HAS A FAMOUS technique internally for product design where they start the product design process by looking to the near future and making a launch press release and press conference of the product-to-be. The idea is it helps them distill down to just the most important things to say, or talk about, or make, in the product.

We're going to go even further in the pursuit of innovation-thinking. This approach goes like this:

> *In the future - 60-80 years from now, what would a historian of that time look back at as the one big thing that changed everything?*

(Disclaimer: We are still assuming A.I. hasn't wiped us off by then).

Using this approach in an actual brainstorming session seems silly, but it can often have a profound impact on innovation-thinking and solution development, particularly when finding that big picture about the type of product or company to build, or finding substantial features to add in a product, or finding substantial problems to aim to solve.

This is because this method brushes away any solution that - while promising for current-day demand - would be insignificant to that future history. The niche things, things like getting your car a car-wash appointment, or that customer-support tool with twitter integration, or the photo apps with new types of party filters.

This helps to focus on things that complete this sentence from that future historian:

> *People used to do _____ once, but then*
> *_____ came along, and it changed*
> *_____.*

Big things, that are remembered (and taken for granted) decades later.

E.g. "People on the internet used to act like monstrous trolls once, but then <this> came along, and changed everything. Thought-provoking discourse at global scale became possible, and in just three years, we fixed global warming, won the first chess-match against A.I., and made coffee free for all."

I'm making light of this, but I do genuinely believe this technique helps to find solutions that focus on very specific meaningful change for the world.

Solutions that unlock the barriers to progress for the human race. That focus on macro-economic change towards improvement. On seemingly complex and inter-linked problems in need of much cleaner solutions. That find "gateway technology" to build, the type that once made, then enables innovative solutions not possible before them.

Here are some more freebies:

"Farmers in <countries here> once had to haggle with tough middlemen that ate away 95% of their profits, but that was until <this> came along. That allowed farmers to sell direct to customers at internet scale at a quarter of market prices, and this rapidly made possible more equitable food distribution around the world, leading to the eventual end of world hunger."

"People's credit-worthiness used to be determined by a complex process controlled by banks and credit card companies, determined by their ability to pay back loans and oddly also their ability to hold loans. But then <this> came along, and everything got better - people's credit-worthiness became a much more transparent process, more easily rewarding people who did great financial planning. In the years since, this increased per-capita spending by X%, boosting economic growth by Y%"

The example above doesn't need to be a complex or ambitious system - it can just be a simple web-based thing. But the solution is where that value lies.

Now, granted you are quite literally planning over an 80 year time-frame, which sounds absurd for any startup or new product or initiative.

But you're also doing more than simply making a mission statement. You are creating a very specific framing of how a specific solution can have a specific possible impact, with the application of a specific amount of ambition.

If nothing else, it's going to build a certain type of focus and energy - a level of motivation that permeates to all layers of the work you and your team does.

And it makes for targets, goals and ideas worth discussing, worth considering, worth paying attention to. And it makes for audacity worth supporting.

7 THE FUNDAMENTAL ASSUMPTION

THIS ONE IS QUICK and easy. It is similar to first-principles but easier to reason through.

It goes like this:

> "What is the fundamental assumption
> that everyone keeps making whenever
> they make a product of this type - and
> what if that fundamental assumption was
> changed. What would happen then - can
> that make better solutions?"

Here are a few fundamental assumptions that are ripe for change:

- Calendars are supposed to have 30 boxes;

- Displays are (sortof) supposed to be based on RGB pixels;

- Setting a time means you should be given an alarm sound when it's time;

- Interfaces are supposed to be driven by buttons or mice [this was the fundamental assumption changed with touch/ gestures].

Change those assumptions, and radical innovation is likely to follow.

8 BACK TO THE CUSTOMER

THIS IS A METHOD introduced to me in the excellent book "UN-LEASHING THE KILLER APP: DIGITAL STRATEGIES FOR MARKET DOMI-NANCE"[1] by Larry Downes and Chunka Mui. I'd highly recommend the book.

They were explaining what the business-case for websites and e-commerce sites was and why businesses and investors were so bullish on e-commerce (this was published in April 1998 by the way, the height of the dot-com boom).

They explained it as websites help retail stores essentially "outsource customer service back to customers", thereby

---

1   "Unleashing the Killer App: Digital Strategies for Market Dominance", Amazon.com, March 2000. http://www.amazon.com/Unleashing-Killer-App-Strategies-Dominance/dp/1578512611

removing that cost-function from their own operations, allowing for items to be cheaper and profits to be higher.

That framework of how to view a website stuck in my mind, and I've since realized that that thinking can be applied to pretty much any operations function at a company, consistently yielding highly innovative new solutions that can greatly improve a company's overall competitiveness.

Here's the method: you pick a typical successful company or dominant player in a typical industry. Then ask yourself: "If we build a company offering the same thing in the same industry, what parts of the company or product or business or workflows could I outsource back to customers?"

"Outsource to customers" isn't a very accurate or positive representation of what's happening - it diminishes the contributions of a community of customers that are willing to be an engaged participant with your company, a believer in the overall vision that everyone is heading towards. That participation is essential for companies like this to exist - a better phrasing would be "what business functions can the community help us with in this type of business?".

The phrasing "outsourcing to customer" only helps to frame how this affects the cost / operations side, only used as a thinking-model.

What I find most interesting though, is this isn't innovation through offering a product that is drastically better, but it's innovation through a drastically better operations model or value-chain. It lets you offer the same product at such a drastically reduced cost or such a more efficient value-chain that it gives you a permanent price, value or speed advantage.

And because of social media, the general willingness of the crowd to work with companies they like, and more power shifting back to consumers, it is becoming easier and more possible every day to have people choose to be a larger part of the vision of your company.

Let's look at a few examples of how this framework of thinking can apply to different companies and their operational models.

Quirky was a bold concept for consumer electronics companies [Update! During the process of writing this book, Quirky filed for bankruptcy - see how quickly information changes?]. It took a traditional consumer-electronics brand business and outsourced product design of its products out to customers. It was designed around the community coming together and pitching physical product ideas, the community evolving and building interest on those ideas, and Quirky taking care of the production, shipping, manufacturing logistics to get those products shipped back to the same community. All of those things were good, and not the reasons for the bankruptcy. I think it was just out-executed by other companies like GE, and couldn't get volumes high enough to get pricing for what would make sense for those products (and a few other things too long to elaborate on here).

Another example of this would be Threadless, and marketplace companies to a smaller extent (for example Evanto).

Digg was a newspaper that outsourced editorial review of the relevance of news to the community (immensely useful, but eventually susceptible to gaming). I don't count Reddit in the same category as they were always different.

YouTube takes a typical media network business and outsources content production, scheduling, curation and promotion out to customers. It takes care of content syndication, broadcasting and advertising.

AirBnB and Lyft take a hotels and taxi business and outsource asset and inventory management back out to customers, essentially having an infinitely scalable pool of stay or travel options available to customers.

Companies like Firefox and others that have open-source as one of the their key pillars are effectively outsourcing development to the community, keeping overall project management, product management and support internal.

Wikipedia outsourced content writing, editing, upkeep and more out to the community.

Companies like SuperTaskers, Scriptd, and to an extent 99Designs and Kaggle are effectively outsourcing HR / hiring / team-building to the community (depending on whether you see them as a marketplace or a company you're hiring.)

Minecraft and several videogames outsource level-design responsibility to the community. Some physical social experiments, like the "Watch the Skies" mass-game held in the U.K. annually, tries to use the community for strategic thinking and planning.

Many companies push "Product Discovery" and "Roadmap Planning" back out to customers through portals that let people discuss, upvote and evolve product ideas together. Dell and Sony are some of the larger firms that have done this to moderate successes, and many startups do this often.

These examples, however, are mostly general, and mostly relating to crowdsourcing. This thinking-method is about figuring out how to implement this in very specific industries, and primarily to offset operational costs. For example, the book publishing industry, in particular, is ripe for a publisher that designs its internal operations in that fundamentally different way, that involves the community to speed up the typical publishing cycle. The cost-efficiency that could result isn't just a good to have but essential for competitiveness in the book publishing industry, given how book sales and revenue is trending.

Or picture the retail industry and the future of the in-store experience through a model around this.

It actually isn't limited to operations of a company either - parts of your product could be something that's enhanced, made better, or only made possible by community participation.

Considering all the possible opportunities for innovation using this method, in every industry (from food and retail, fashion and accessories, gadgets and software, media and entertainment, physical spaces, office suites, etc), I always try and use this thinking-method first in consulting projects or startup mentoring and its nearly always resulted in product designs or concepts that are scalable and more interesting and competitive than other players in that market.

9 TAFAKKAR: AN INNOVATION-THINKING METHOD

TAFAKKAR IS A WORD that translates to *deep reflection* - to think on a subject deeply, systematically, and in great detail. It is also the name of a thinking discipline - a specific reflective contemplation technique - that can be used to make more discoveries about the world around you.

The technique is heavily encouraged in, and comes from the religion of Islam. Don't worry, you won't need to learn Islam, or any other religion, in order to understand it. We can still talk about a practice of thought described in it to apply it towards innovation-thinking.

In many ways, Tafakkar is similar to the Scientific Method. It is about these main things:

1. Look at the world around you and pay attention to the very small details.

2. Don't just see what you're immediately seeing, but try to see the system in play behind the thing you're seeing.

3. Once you see that system, try to find the system in play behind that system, and on and on.

This approach can be used to discover new knowledge only through philosophy and reflection, without prior education about something.

For example, imagine someone sees the world around him and sees the trees move. But he also sees other things around the trees, like shrubs or signposts, also get affected consistently. So through reflection he determines there must an invisible force at play moving everything, the wind. Then he can think about what systems are causing the wind to exist, helping him to build an understanding of atmospheric conditions and changes that cause it, from there he can think about what causes the atmosphere to change, and on and on. All this without any prior formal education about that subject.

Or you might notice the layer in between the outer and inner shell of the Date fruit and wonder about its purpose. Or you could look at bees and their organized daily cycle, why only female bees make honey, and the benefits of honey, etc.

On the religion side, the idea is this thought process of discovery would eventually lead to the thinker finding spirituality and evidence of the divine.

But Tafakkar can be applied to anything, not just the physical world - from events or people, to maths and economics, or social or political behavior, to trends.

We're going to use Tafakkar for innovation-thinking. For that, we have to apply it to three things in particular: human, economic and consumer behavior in whatever industry you're aiming to do innovation in.

E.g. you might notice that people tend to react in a particular way to a particular pricing strategy for a certain type of products, and start to think about why. That leads to a better understanding of the history of products in that space, to psychology and the consumer purchase decision model. Then you think about what things could affect that decision model, and start to understand macro or micro-economic influences, or the base desires of people related to wanting to lead a happy life.

You may notice a small detail - some of your blog commenters just started replying to other commenters. And you realize that's never happened before, where everyone was just commenting out to you previously. You start to think about why, leading to a larger understanding of communities and social behavior, which on a deeper layer helps you understand what people want from social interaction to begin with (validation, acceptance etc).

Every time you apply this thinking, you will arm yourself with insight, which can then lead to you doing more profound things compared to how you were before. For example, you could use that knowledge of social interaction in communities to build new marketing techniques focused on community and tribe management.

Or that understanding of the purchase decision model and its influences helps you innovate on the pricing strategy for your company.

The larger point is, by applying this method, you choose to go forth and make decisions not based on what books you've read (ahem!) or what the experts are saying you should do (ahem?), or how everyone else does it.

You don't go forward based on what you think data is telling you at face-value.

You go forth based on understanding.

Based on abstract or economic modelling of underlying behavior and systems.

And sometimes, it helps you truly become a contrarian genius. Because everyone might be looking at the data wrong - seeing declining revenue in some industry, dooming it, writing it off. But you sit on top of the roof, looking down at the masses, and whisper: "no".

(Did you get the movie reference?)

You'll whisper "No," because your understanding of the system tells you the decline is temporary, and reversible, and it just needs this particular software or solution to make it trend up again.

With understanding, you stop chasing trends and start making them.

10 THE CONTEXT OF THE LAST CHANGE

I LOVE SCIENCE-FICTION. ALMOST AS much as I love coffee (Umm - actually no, it's not even close).

But I love science-fiction *writing* whenever time allows (stealth startup - it refuses to allow.) Okay, this segue isn't going anywhere.

There was a time when science-fiction books were just 80 pages or so. Nowadays, they are expected to be epic 400-page tomes in 12-part series.

There's a specific business and market context for both of these changes.

They were eighty pages before primarily because of how they used to be sold on racks in supermarkets, and it was the retail industry heavily pushing for that size so more books could fit on that rack.

They grew to 400 for various reasons you can find on-line. The reasons include inflation, and the rise of hardcovers once Barnes and Nobles and dedicated book sellers replaced supermarkets as the primary distribution leg.

Yet, this is all forgotten in time. We tend to view the present outside of the context that brought us to the present. Devoid of that context, it's easy to imagine that the present is how it's always been, or it's easy to take a request from a publisher or investor or customer at face-value without discussion of other, more interesting or innovative options.

And devoid of interesting options, attention economics says customers and consumers will get less interested in the same stuff over time, making the industry trend downwards.

But, by looking at the context, we can start to say "OK what was the market situation / industry like at the time that forced the last change" and we can start to see if the situation has changed since then.

In almost all cases, the context of today doesn't match the context of yesterday, the one that created the last shift to how things work today.

Or in other words, the context of today doesn't match how things work today.

That creates a gap primed for innovation-thinkers to

jump into.

And sometimes it works out, that the way things used to work in the past can be brought back, because the market context of that really old time actually matches more with the present.

Continuing with the books example, take serialized storytelling - written stories that worked like TV shows with seasons and episodes. They were big in late 19th / early 20th century (e.g. Sherlock Holmes), but for various market and business reasons they disappeared (mostly the cost of distribution).

But today, they'd be a rather "innovative" answer to the book industry's status quo. Market dynamics are different now, making them viable again, because of lower distribution and publishing costs, subscription models, etc. A company, STERLING AND STONE[1], is doing exactly that to create the "HBO of books", and is considered to be doing an innovative thing that advances the publishing industry forward.

---

[1]   "Sterling and Stone", Accessed Jan 4, 2016. https://sterlingandstone.net

11 WHAT IF HISTORY NEVER HAPPENED?

THERE ARE MOMENTS IN history when things get decided and standardized for one reason or another, and it influences decades of products and decisions made after that, all one on top of the other. Usually these moments lie around the time when the first type of some product or discipline was being made.

The first designers had to go through a completely different type of design process compared to the products that came after, since the products made after were just imitating, or building on top of, or deriving from, that original.

Over time - say 20-100 years later - all those original design choices are just assumed as law - all products of this type now must have these basic features, because what do you mean "no"?

The problem is, those first decisions were made for the situation of that era or time, and it may not apply to now.

To innovate, we have to act like the first designers. This has been seen throughout history in "curve jumping" moments - when people ignored all the assumptions and baggage of history to re-make something for the first time.

This is different from the "context of last change" method because you're not looking at market dynamics, but just acting as product designers to ask:

> *What if that history had never happened? What if we were making the first solution, ever. There's no reference, nobody knows what a thing like this should be or should look like. All we know is people have some unmet problems. So what makes sense as a solution, given: (1) how the world is today (2) the technologies we have access to today?*

Say we're applying this thinking to create a task-management app.

Does a task-management app even need the concept of checklists? That's just an industrial-age concept. Do things need check-boxes and a title next to them? All that people are trying to do is refocus their attention on the right priorities and get a sense of how it's coming along.

What type of work are people trying to prioritize today? Does that work really go through two states (checked or not checked)? Does the priority list always get made the same way or changes with certain modern circumstances? What type of actions are related to such a priority list? What cases move things from checked to unchecked to back, or to some other state?

The added overlay on this thought exercise is taking a fresh look at how the world is today - clearly many people aren't doing industrial-age work now. And their work isn't static or deterministic at the start. And those people aren't all in the same building or room, and those people have very different aspirations from their career, and those people have a lot more pressures on their attention all the time.... (on and on...)

The other part of this, that really helps with innovation, is "given the technologies available today" part. A lot of the old-guard ways of doing things are quite often just based on the limitations of technologies or systems available at the time. Many typography rules for example are still carrying forward restrictions on how the printing press had to be originally designed, how blocks of lead was added to space out lines and keep text on a grid.

All modern user-interfaces are designed primarily around the two dimensional restrictions of a display and

X-Y mouse system. With VR, why should interfaces still be flat things, now just floating in the air? (Or conversely, why would they just be surrounding you in weird 3d objects) - why wouldn't they use the spatial awareness features of VR to full advantage? What should "movies in VR" do to deal with fast-cuts and edits in a scene - does a "movie" analogy even have to work, or is VR suited for its own unique medium with its own rules for storytelling?

There is lots of room for fun, innovative solutions if we just assume history never happened and we are the first designers of something.

One addendum: Just keep in mind, when you take solutions like that back to customers, they wouldn't have gone through that same thought process - so customers will always expect solutions based on a reference of whatever they're already familiar with. And sometimes if you're truly innovating, you have to be prepared for some investment in re-education or bringing customers along in the thinking process of innovation as well.

Another addendum: This approach isn't best for every single small thing you'll do. It's meant for the big things, like what the overall structure or philosophy or design ethos of a product is going to be. Sometimes you just have to lock down that design and get building fast. If you find yourself wistfully wondering "Is a button really a button?", you may have gone too far into the deep end of a coffee mug.

12 ORIGINAL INTENT THINKING

ONE THING I'VE FOUND, is that when people live in a certain status quo long enough, they start to forget what they originally set out to do. "Its always been this way" becomes the way of thinking and it stalls innovation.

It's because they set out to find some original solution - their original intent. What they were *actually wanting to do*. But at some point they settle for the only *current available option*. And, given enough time, they forget what they were originally aiming to do. We're talking about a 100 or so years in terms of time in some cases.

It is useful then in problem discovery to use this line of reasoning to find good solutions:

What is this person's Original Intent?
What is this person actually wanting to do
for which he or she is currently doing this?

Often you find that there are many parts of what they're originally wanting to do that are still unmet.

Companies for example, when hiring, aren't wanting to gather job applicants or their resumes, nor collect any test answers, nor collect solutions to projects or challenges sent to the applicants. They're actually just wanting to find someone who matches their values, demonstrates the willingness to adapt to and tackle new challenges, and demonstrates the maturity and ethics to want to keep the companies interests at the forefront. And applicants aren't wanting to do that dance either, they're just wanting to find a great place to work at that matches their values, enables them to do their best work, and makes their time there an enjoyable and rewarding experience for their career.

All of the things companies and applicants currently do in the recruiting process is just their current best way of reaching towards their original intent, but it is still a far-cry from the ideal.

Fictional storytellers aren't actually wanting to write books, or novels, or use any other medium. They actually have a picture - a 3-dimensional moving scene, often with dialog and music and camera cuts and facial expressions and clothing and special effects - of what they want to convey, in their minds, and the process of writing text is the only best way they currently know of translating that into a medium others can understand. But there's a huge gap between the picture that's made in the mind of the reader and the one in the mind of the writer.

Programmers aren't actually wanting to write complex, inaccessible code linearly file after file, jumping through dozens of hoops and check-in systems to get anything done. They don't even want to be discussing on Hacker News how *their way* of jumping through those hoops is *the best one.* There's no pride in needless cognitive exhaustion. Their Original Intent is they want to create an abstract model about the constraints and logic and data processing that a system should implement in order to reliably do what it's meant to, and they want it implemented in a lowest-total-lifecycle-cost way. And programming languages, compilers, databases, and everything else they currently use is just the current option to do that based on how file-systems, checkin-tools, test-automation tools, deployment tools, computer processors and memory-designs *currently* work.

Journalists aren't actually looking for task-tools, or better phones or better cameras or a replacement to email. They're looking for ways to break news faster, at higher quality, with more insights, to increase their readership. That's their Original Intent.

Blogs aren't about having a piece of text with comments below it, and discourse isn't about better forum software. Its about offering a point of view, then hearing additive or counter points of view in a way that creates a bigger understanding of the thing being discussed, while diminishing noise and unproductive forces.

People aren't looking for faster horses. They want a more efficient way of getting from A to B in a manner of their choosing.

It goes on and on.

Everything past the Original Intent is up for change or a rethink. Whoever can make a better way for journalists to break news faster and increase their readership will get them to drop their current systems, no matter how big or successful or ingrained those current products may seem to be. Whoever makes a better solution for online discourse involving points of view will solve the internet trolls problem. Whoever makes a new way of telling fiction stories that is much closer to conveying that picture in mind for storytellers, would expand the market, inspiring generations of new writers to start telling stories. Whoever makes a solution for travel better than a faster horse, people will use it even if it has worse UI (which cars did).

Whenever you make a solution that gets people closer to their Original Intent, they'll be quick to drop whatever current products or systems they use to get there. There's no "hard to get people to change" when its going closer to Original Intent. You just have to seek the Original Intent first, then go forward from there.

Keep one thing in mind though, any radical rethink forward from the Original Intent isn't the type of solution you can quickly hash together on a weekend, start customer ~~discovery~~ sales on and do incremental and iterative improvement on. Lean methods won't quite get you there.

Original Intents are age-old problems that have always been, whose demand is constant, well-known, timeless and unwavering and will always remain in the future. New, radical solutions to age-old problems need to be comprehensive, and sure in themselves. They can't go closer to the Original Intent halfheartedly. They need to be built with patience, and thoroughness. In essence, you can't try to make something to replace faster horses by making a car without a steering wheel, nor by starting with a skateboard.

This type of innovation requires the support of a particular type of investor, who is in it for the long-term, who is focused on expanding and creating markets and changing industries and focused on valuation and growth, and who wants to support the innovator and entrepreneur's vision and is on board with what they're aiming to do.

But to me, solutions created using Original Intent Thinking also present the least risk. They are the ones that are most stable, get to be first-to-market in that next curve-jump, get the most attention and sustained mind-share, make the most competitors sweat, make the most customers feel surprised or delighted... and in my mind these are the types of things that create high-growth companies, not whether every assumption is data-verified.

13 THE LHO

So IMAGINE WHATEVER CUSTOMERS are buying today, in an industry, to not be something they're satisfied with, but the *Least Happy Option* (LHO) available to them for what they need (also known as a Minimum Viable Product - *just kidding!*).

As a thought exercise, if you imagine customers currently just barely tolerating whatever products exist in the market, that can sometimes be a motivating force for you to want to improve their lives through something better.

And the last thing it makes you want to do is make the same thing as the least-happy-option.

And it forces a certain exploratory method of figuring out what actually would make them happier and *even more* satisfied. That had better be substantially more satisfying or delightful than the current thing.

This doesn't always yield something innovative or interesting, and is a rather pessimistic view of the world, but sometimes just a simple thought-experiment like that can work in recharging our own internal motivation for change.

14 FORCE THE INNOVATOR'S DILEMMA ON COMPETITORS

THE INNOVATOR'S DILEMMA[1] IS one of those really well-known concepts that has a lot of material you can find online. I'd highly recommend the book if you're unfamiliar with it. Here though, let's just focus on how to use our understanding of it to do innovation-thinking.

The concept we'll understand from it is that large successful incumbents can have a hard time investing in products that will cannibalize their existing core business-lines. It is

---

1   "The Innovator's Dilemma: The Revolutionary Book That Will Change the Way You Do Business", Amazon.com. Oct 4, 2011. http://www.amazon.com/The-Innovators-Dilemma-Revolutionary-Business/dp/0062060244

very hard to get leadership and board and shareholder buy-in to kill the things that are making the majority of a company's profits, stability and income, just because there is a newer, untested, unproven way to be explored.

Usually that paves the path for newer startups to come in and challenge those incumbents. The classic examples here are Netflix and Redbox out-competing Blockbuster Video - you can look these examples up online, and frankly read the book in its entirety.

Okay so, given that, how do we build an innovation-thinking discipline that helps us build great things?

Well, thinking strategically, this comes down to asking "What can we make, and how do we position it in the market, that makes it impossible for incumbents to follow without killing themselves?"

It's actually about as simple as it sounds. For entrepreneurship, the sequence of steps would be

1. Decide to build a company in an industry you deeply understand, where you can see stubborn incumbents, and can clearly see better and more interesting solutions

2. In deciding product options or feature options, find a spot which incumbents could not announce without it affecting the sales of their existing core products.

Finding such a spot can come from looking at their marketing. If there's one thing larger companies worry about more than their product line, it's brand perception. The last thing they'll often want is to muddle up the message of who they are and what they offer, or confusing the user into thinking the company isn't really sure what solution is the correct one. That can have significant additive negative affects on sales of all their product-lines and impact trust on all their future announcements.

So extending from that reasoning, an incumbent cannot announce something that contradicts the marketing message they're already making about their existing products, or is going to put them at contention with what their existing customers trust or believe.

As a simplified theoretical example: (Pre-Hindenburg), any company that bet everything on a profitable hydrogen or helium airship line of products, built on the argument that "luxury in the air" is the way of the future, will have a hard time competing with a contradictory message from challengers that "speed and economy in the air is the way to go" with more modern jet-engine airplanes. So those two would be placed in such a way where one cannot chase the other.

"Forcing the Innovator's Dilemma" as a thinking method is about finding and discovering that sweet spot that will polarize an incumbent's existing customer base and build a market behind a wall they're unable to cross, for reputation or profit reasons. It can yield solutions that end up with markets that have people hungry for change, that have no competition and all the upside to grab, which is a great place for entrepreneurs and investors alike.

But also be aware: Enterprise companies and incumbents today have gotten a lot smarter about managing the Innovator's Dilemma.

They will spin-out more risky and experimental things into a separate brand altogether, which removes the risk of cannibalization. You can see this approach with hotel chains (pre AirBnB) making smaller off-shoot brands like Homewood Suites (Hilton), Hyatt House (Hyatt), or restaurants experimenting with upmarket trendy brands like THE DEN[2] (Denny's) and THE RESERVE ROASTERY[3] (Starbucks).

More significantly, almost every enterprise company we've worked with the past few years has been scrambling to set up and build "innovation centers" internally. These are built with advice from either people like me who have experience in startup support communities, or people with expertise in setting up coworking environments (e.g. my good friends at OPENWORK[4]). They are designed to work like accelerators and

---

2   "Denny's targets Millennials with 'The Den'", Nation's Restaurant News, Mar 9, 2015. http://nrn.com/casual-dining/denny-s-targets-millennials-den

3   "Starbucks Reserve: Roastery and Tasting Room", Starbucks. Accessed Jan 4, 2016. http://roastery.starbucks.com/

4   "OpenWork: Evolve the Marketplace", OpenWork.com, Accessed Jan 4, 2016. http://openwork.agency/

incubators inside of the enterprise, with (potentially) all the funding and support of the large enterprise, and a faster and simpler pitching and negotiating process for their incubated "startups".

They are also experimenting with new business models to facilitate continuous innovation. E.g. Sony's FIRST FLIGHT[5] crowdsourcing site, which enables it's employees to make more experimental offerings and see which garner interest.

If anything then, the enterprises that execute this correctly over the next 5-10 years - being better funded and potentially faster than startups at getting things made and getting the word out - can be a formidable force of innovation, requiring startups to horizontally integrate to offer something similar. The closest we have of such enterprises are the Googles and Facebooks and such "startup" oriented giant companies of the world.

However, in general, that time isn't now, or here. And many of those innovation centers or approaches in enterprise companies will initially be small steps, half-baked attempts, or focused only on expanding on their existing core product lines (e.g. building better airships). And there is work to be done before their internal pitching and negotiation process gets faster than the startup world. Not to mention the operational flexibility that comes from horizontal integration that enterprises

---

5   "The First Flight", Sony, Accessed Jan 4, 2016. https://first-flight.sony. com/

would need to build to try radically different things.

Until then, there are always opportunities to find that wall, that market those larger, more successful incumbents are unable to venture into without killing their core products or marketing message. And that can be a direction to steer towards for more innovative solutions.

15 ASSUME YOUR CUSTOMERS ALREADY HAVE YOUR COMPETITORS PRODUCT

A LOT OF COMPANIES REMAIN too fixated on competitors, in ways that only result in 10-20% improvement over them.

One thing I've sadly heard too many times, is (paraphrased) "well the competitor has feature X, hence feature X is probably important" - except most of those competitors are also just looking around for ideas for what to add rather than really doing product discovery.

Sometimes this problem of looking only to improve over competition comes from the culture of innovation and startups. If every conversation starts with "Whats the idea?" or "Who do you compete against?", or "What is your competitive advantage?" , the conversations and thought process tends to become too competitor focused. A better conversation starter for innovators would be "What's the problem you're passionate about, and why?"

I started doing the following thought-experiment to help reframe the thinking for entrepreneurs who were too competitor focused, to get them focused on the right goals. To go from "competitive advantages" - the 10-20% improvement over competition - to "disruptive advantage".

Here's how this works:

Assume your customer already has purchased your closest, best competitor, the one you're afraid of most. If it's software: try and imagine that that software is sitting open in front of them *right now*, and the customer has a dreamy-eyed, beaming smile on their face looking at it, as if they were in love.

See? Now there's no chance any competitive advantage will make a difference. Their total cost of acquiring the competitors product (buying + transitioning + learning cost) is zero.

On the other hand, your product represents a huge acquisition cost in moving away from the product they love, buying your product, transitioning data, learning and training everyone on it, etc.

Sufficiently depressed?

Good. So, now what? **What can you offer NOW - that despite them having that software open in front of them with all their data - they *still* want to move to you?**

That's disruptive advantage.

And the way to finding the answer is to go one-step deeper in understanding what the customer wants - *really wants* - the things they want that they haven't even said they want, but will probably need. Or the things that will surprise them in saying: "Oh I didn't know that was something that could be done, this will certainly help me in much better ways".

What's the customer's actual core problem that he's not even thinking about?

Find that, and you'll get to the level of clarity Henry Ford had when he said "If I'd asked them what they'd wanted, they would have said a faster horse."

16 THE NEGATIVE SPACE OF POSSIBILITY

THE PRESENT IS LIMITED. Cursed to describe only how things are today; what products people are using today; what activities they're doing today; how they're engaging with things today. That's boring.

The problem with the present is it creates a false proxy for demand: what people are currently using doesn't necessarily correlate with them wanting to use that thing, as I've already touched on a few times in this book. It doesn't say much about whether said thing is the best thing they could possibly use, should a better option exist. Most people always pick the better option, once available. And that game, the one about finding the better option that's not yet available, and making it available… that's not boring.

Sometimes, for innovation-thinking, what people are doing today or even wanting today isn't an interesting enough question. What's more interesting as a question or puzzle is what people are not doing today, and the context for why that is.

The key question to ask when finding better solutions is:

What is the negative space of possibility around these users or markets?

What people are *currently using* isn't as interesting as what they want to, or should be using to make their lives drastically better. Instead of "they are using this [limited product] hence they probably want [limited products]" the negative space has a better question: "What are the things people are not able to do with the [limited products] that they've wanted to, and why aren't they able to find any product to fit that gap?"

How people are *currently* coming to your webpage, and the conversion rate for your product isn't entirely interesting. Too often people get obsessed about that out of desperation or pressure, and spend all their available time converting a 3% conversion rate to a 5% with obsessive A/B testing or tweaks or growth hacking. The negative space has a better question: "Why aren't 80% of the people who end up on our site able to convert? What's driving away the 60th percentile?" Those are challenging, fundamental questions that would either reveal deep product problems, or reveal over-spending on the wrong marketing channels that are resulting in poorly qualified leads.

How many of a certain type of customers there are in a market isn't interesting enough. It doesn't matter to an innovation-thinker that there're about six million screenwriters in the world. The negative space has a better question: "Why isn't everyone a screenwriter? What's stopping more stories from being written, and more movies from being made (other than interest)? What's getting in the way of young children aspiring to be screenwriters, or in the way of emerging screenwriters from getting a chance to prove themselves?" There are atleast a dozen new innovative, disruptive, meaningful companies hidden in the answers to those questions.

The fact that dozens or hundreds of people or companies failed at a certain market in the past doesn't matter. The negative space has a better question: "How can the next company be poised to do what no one could? What could they see that all the others missed? What strong beliefs or insights would they build upon that no one else seems to have the context to believe?" Those are the opportunities worth pursuing.

How much of the market a competitor is capturing is less interesting than how much of the market is still left open, or how much of the market they're missing.

How easy things are now isn't as interesting as how

much easier they still could be.

What conventions we must follow when building or making a certain type of thing is less interesting than the conventions we could break to offer something better.

Too much conversation in the startup / business world is based on what's hot today, chasing a trend that's already formed. Yet so much of the companies that disrupt and challenge markets is about seeing the trend or the thing that no one is seeing right now. For which there isn't data yet, because what you're making might be a worlds-first.

Many businesses chase the space that already exists, the one that offers the comfort of safe answers. Innovation-thinkers chase the negative space around it in the pursuit of better answers.

17 RE-APPLY FOUNDING VISION

THERE IS SOMETHING VERY powerful about the founding moments of a project, initiative or company. It is those moments that are unbridled by the burdens of reality, of budgets or restrictions or limits or stresses, but are only about possibility, of the future and the change and betterment that that initiative may bring.

The founding moments capture the intent and vision of founders and the instigators of that venture in a way that few other things do, and especially in ways that are often very hard to find or discover later on.

And that original vision is what makes a lot of these companies just work. That vision attracts people who share it and want to do something about it. It attracts customers who want to be a part of that change. That's because those companies are setting out on a mission, to right some wrong or to improve the human condition in some way.

Over time, business realities and interests get in the way and often contend with that vision.

But historically, it seems the companies that hold true to that vision as much as they can through the years, tend to continue to attract the best talent and customers and continue to grow. And the companies that don't, the ones that perhaps add too much business influence from people who weren't the original founders, they tend to sometimes change things so drastically that their customers and original supporters are no longer able to see that same vision they got on board for, causing them to leave.

The fascinating part of this is even if the company ends up doing something entirely different, as long as it is keeping in with the original vision, customers tend to carry forward positively to the change because they still see that signature essence.

So for innovation-thinking, sometimes it's useful to look at whether or not that vision of the founding members of the company could be interpreted in newer and more interesting ways, for newer business lines. Democracies do that all the time, but companies can as well.

I like the example of Nintendo Corporation. That company currently is focused on the video-games market - you might know of them because of Mario or the Wii or something. But it's impressive to realize Nintendo is a 126-year old company with its roots in 1889 - that's Victorian era / the Wild West / mid-industrial age by the way - starting as a hand-made playing cards company. And it's interesting to read how they tried many things - a Taxi company, a hotel company, a food network - eventually moving into toys and family entertainment closer to their original vision - first making light-guns and arcades, to game and watch systems to home entertainment to mobile entertainment onward. Throughout this time, they've held firm to the core Nintendo beliefs. Not just to deliver bundles of family-friendly fun, but to do it in a fully-integrated way (all hardware / content production in-house) and to keep all operational / business details hidden from their public message, which is just about entertainment.

Another example is Disney, which has continued to reinterpret Walt Disney's vision of entertainment through characters in interesting new ways. Their work in theme parks, purchasing Pixar and Marvel and Lucasfilm all serves that larger mission of character-based entertainment for families, and that's what keeps Disney fans and customers engaged and in sync.

You could say Facebook has been decently good at reinterpreting their core mission to enable better social connections between people, with their purchases of Instagram, WhatsApp and Oculus.

And Google's best projects have come from following their vision of tackling things that require the organization of information at global scale.

This innovation-thinking method mostly applies to larger companies, or startup teams who've been operating for a while, but its a great way to staying ahead of the Innovator's Dilemma - to try to find the soul of the company that was seeded in its formative years and bring out a fresh take on it.

Of course there are lots of specific business decisions and demand indicators and numbers and dollars behind all of those changes, but the original vision keeps the perception of the company stable and consistent on the things that made customers fall in love with it to begin with.

18 STAY ON THE EDGES OF YOUR INDUSTRY

ALL INDUSTRIES – INCLUDING the startup "industry" now - develop culture, and hence a status quo about how everyone is supposed to do things, because that's how it has always been or how it is socially acceptable. Social behaviors and activities form, that are considered "normal", that outsiders start thinking of conforming to in order to be socially accepted.

It builds ~~"best practice"~~ "current practice" around everything (there's no such thing as "best practice" for innovation-thinkers).

All this adds a layer of inertia for innovators or contrarian thinkers to have to push through to get anything done. Industry politics and culture can become an anchor that weighs down all idea creation, or innovation-thinking or decision making, all fundraising or budget-getting, all allocation of focus and time.

I've found it is rather essential for innovation-thinking, that a company should not get too engrossed in the daily minutia of the industry it's serving or the ones it's a part of. It helps to stay just on the edges, enough to be aware of "current practices", but enough to be out of the day-to-day politics about how things are expected to be done.

This stuck out from a Star Wars documentary, that described George Lucas wanting to stay just at the edges of the film industry when making the first Star Wars film, to not be burdened too much by the industry's influence. The early key people at ILM (and many people after) were all hired from outside of the film industry. And that helped them change everything about how things were supposed to be done, from non-linear film editing, to compositing, to sound production, to movie theatre design, special effects, marketing through merchandising, and much more.

The games industry is currently stuck deeply on how a AAA game is *supposed* to be marketed, or produced, or mar-ket-tested. The book industry has its own set notions of what a book is *supposed* to be, how big it should be, how it should be launched, how the awards circuit or best-seller lists work, how to look at and treat "fans" or readers of books, etc.

What slows things down if we're too deep in particu-lar industries is conversations about innovation, because the participants quite often aren't able to see a world outside of the world they're familiar with, or are too concerned about the feathers they might ruffle or the relationships they might affect or the boats they might rock.

This even affects people whose job is creative thinking. Quite often people can get too insular in the day-to-day approaches to product design. They get so vested in being a part of the Tech industry that all the "good" or "bad" ideas of the design of products or the design of businesses around the products, come from within the bubble of socially accepted norms they might be in (the very limited and specific norms of the specific industry they might be in). I've seen this all too often in startups, founders, in engineers or design teams, or even larger companies. "Person X from <some other company doing some other thing> said approach Y is how its *supposed to be done*".

When you sit on the edge of an industry, you're able to retain an outside perspective on that industry, since you don't ever have to agree with the majority view just for social acceptance reasons. You're able to remain objective about what's working and what isn't, and you're able to find the type of critical thinking that can lead to a better place of improvement for that industry.

What's more, I've found it helpful to stay at the edge of several industries, and to step out and look for inspiration or ideas from what those other industries are doing. You can take ideas that are working really well in one industry, and start to apply them to another, and localized to that other industry, they'll create innovative new solutions. I'm often surprised that despite the internet existing and open access to information, more people don't do this, and can be oblivious to things happening month to month in other industries around them.

Some examples:

The games industry learnt a lot about thinking of "software as a service" from freemium business models coming from the Tech software industry around 2007. Conversely, the SAAS software industry can now learn from what the games industry is doing with monetization and transactional income.

The Music industry can teach Tech and Consulting industries a lot about variances of abundance and scarcity and positioning one product to create demand for another.

The Movie industry (specifically the design of the first act of movies) can teach a lot about the art of storytelling and influence the Copywriting and Content Marketing and Presentation Design industries, and even software in the design of the the first-touch moment and tutorials.

The hotels / hospitality industry can teach an immense amount to customer service and software and consumer-tech product design.

The book publishing industry could benefit greatly from some of the ideas happening in the startup industry with incubators, launch landing pages, etc.

The list goes on.

Whenever interesting trends from one industry are applied to another, newer and more magical things are created.

In fact, in general, I find the most insightful knowledge comes from looking at the world through the lens of someone else in the world - other cultures, other industries, other people (and I'm always surprised that this isn't obvious).

Some of the best things I've learnt about product strategy have come from talking to road-side street vendors selling vegetables in Pakistan. My teams used insights from film compositing to better understand typography and presentation design, or from horror-stories of crunch in game production to help streamline content marketing workflows. The Mbira and Erhu instruments and what they mean to their respective cultures has taught me a lot about pacing in science fiction storytelling. You get the idea.

So, the take-away is: retain an outside perspective on your own industry or the one you're operating in (and be quick to critically analyze what can improve about it) and always be open to outside perspectives from the world beyond your world and your culture and your life, and innovation is likely to follow.

19 META PATTERNS

ONE OF THE GOOD fortunes I had in my early career was to get the chance to have a short stint as an analyst, and in management consulting. Analysts are forced to quickly develop a certain skill that isn't quite taught elsewhere - the ability to very rapidly understand and see macro-level patterns in industries, to build an instinct on how an industry moves and shifts, what the value-chain is and how the money flows, and what things influence it.

It is also true that most analysts are wrong at whatever they try to predict based on that insight. Their job however, isn't quite to predict the future, but to frame what factors may influence some change to come.

Side note: I've long maintained that this skill - the ability to see industry patterns at macro-scale - should be a fundamental skill taught to everyone in college - engineering and business and communication people alike. I have some thoughts on what a course for it could be - maybe a mandatory semester where people have to work with an analyst firm at some really hard stuff. To me this skill is just as fundamental as the ability to deliver presentations, because it is an essential part of how people frame the business justification for any of their pitches or internal ideas at work. End side-note.

Over recent years, I've started noticing something slightly different. Even within the general patterns of macro-change, there are several repeatable and predictable patterns-of-patterns that influence industries, product-innovation, economics and human behavior.

These "Meta Patterns", as I've been calling them, keep coming up as things that govern and dictate how things move from the "old way" to the "new way" in industries. Now, some of these cyclical trends have been observed by other analysts too, but not treated holistically.

What's fascinating about Meta Patterns, is they give you a fairly stable framework to help predict the near-to-mid term future, say about 3-4 years ahead. Or at least some trends in it. This gives you time to start building solutions for that next step of the market. At CDF Software, we've been applying Meta-Pattern Thinking for the various work we do, like strategic decisions, and its been consistently accurate in predicting when certain changes will come into play.

A few other notes before we dive into them.

I'm not sure if Meta Patterns should be considered laws as such (akin to Moore's Law). I don't know how many da-ta-points one has to consider to declare something *laws of change*. But their affect on industries *is* very consistent in all the data-points that I *have* seen (which, for all I know, may be statistically small).

I'm also not sure how many of these there are. About a year ago I started writing down these patterns whenever I'd happen to identify one of them, just to see if there really are enough of these Meta Patterns to take notice of. So far I've found about forty-six of them.

Final disclaimer: I haven't done the research on whether this is all just a well-known branch of economics that I'm just not privy to. If not, maybe it should be.

Okay, so here I'll just cover a couple of them briefly to help you understand Meta Patterns, to get you going on thinking about, observing and discovering more of them. The forty-four others may have to wait for another short-book later on.

Deep jug of coffee now.

PATTERN: THE PREMIUM / COMMODITY CYCLE

> *Whatever is premium today, will be commoditized tomorrow, creating a pathway to the new premium*

THIS IS THE EASIEST to understand. Whatever anyone is offering and is able to charge a premium price for today, will result in driven people around the world pushing themselves to learn how to provide that thing. With increasing supply and competition, and the fact that new players could come from anywhere globally, that premium thing becomes common-place and commodity priced.

At that point, the people who had setup their operations (costs of doing their business) to enjoy or rely on that premium have to rush to either live with declining income, or rapidly reinvent themselves and find that next thing to focus on that can justify the premium.

This is the harsh reality of (or awesome thing about, depending on your perspective) most knowledge work, particularly technical and design work.

The past several years, engineers in web-app development space have been going through this cycle. There was a time when scalable web engineering work was premium priced, but increasingly there are brilliant people all over the world living in lower-cost-of-living environments happy to offer the same quality of service at better cost. Then the top-end went deep into modern web stacks and angular and devops, and eventually everyone else followed, now the top-end of web engineering is deep into dockers and advanced javascript constructs like promises or functional programming, or language design, or machine learning. Eventually more and more people will follow.

The marketing industry has been seeing this at the agency level the past few years. There was a time just about five years ago when content marketing or community development work was premium, then it became common-place. Then integrated marketing strategy became premium, then common-place. Now, many of the marketing firms competing at the top layer are moving upstream - hiring programmers to build custom algorithms or platforms, and moving from marketing strategy towards general product or innovation strategy, often requiring a rebranding of their firms. Some agencies are just shutting down or merging with larger ones.

Side note: It's funny because, the information in this book is just the type of information that agencies are using to provide that premium innovation-strategy work. So this book could have the effect of making the innovation-strategy work more commoditized and common, which could quite literally affect many agencies practicing it, including the agency I founded. Hmm.

You can see this type of shift in many different industries the past few years - the game development industry, book publishing, etc.

The music industry in particular saw a corollary of this - which was "whatever is scarce today will be abundant to-morrow, creating new avenues for scarcity". There was a time when music albums in stores and music videos on TV were scarce and premium, but now they're commodities via iTunes and YouTube. But by embracing the commodity (giving albums away for free), music artists have created more demand for better scarcities (limited seats at concert venues).

By accepting the inevitability of this Meta Pattern, you can get ahead of this curve. Look at whatever is on the "premi-um" side of things today, assume it'll be commoditized within a few years, and then extrapolate to what the next premium is likely to be - typically this means going upstream (or down-stream in the user's natural flow) and finding something that's still "scarce". Then you can build solutions or techniques to get ready for that next era of premium, some of which could take all of those years to do R&D or experimentation on.

For example, looking again at the music industry, it's easy to see that within three years, Virtual Reality could turn concert-venues from a scarcity to an abundance again, and if that happens artists will have to scramble to find something new that is scarce. You (as an entrepreneur) now have a three-year head-start on making something that could be that next premium.

You can use this thinking method when prioritizing feature-development in a product roadmap as well. Features that you consider premium value today will be common tomorrow, creating an impetus for innovation thinking, constantly guiding you towards investments in product that improve competitiveness and relevance.

PATTERN: THE PRODUCTIVITY DANCE BETWEEN TOOLS AND TECHNIQUES

In productivity, the tools we have influences the techniques and methods we use, which influences the tools that are made, which influences the methods we use...

THERE'S AN ENDLESS CYCLE of influence in the productivity domain, that has been the case since the invention of the first tool by primitive Man. For example, only after the creation of the hammer, could one start to understand how to better schedule and streamline work methods to make the best use of the hammer.

On the other hand, a lot of productivity software is built only to serve the needs of particular emerging techniques and methods, e.g. agile project management.

Something I'm always surprised by, is when I meet someone who, for example, believes strongly that a methodology like "agile development" is the only definitive way forward. It might be, sure, *for now*, but it is only the *current best choice* and directly dependent on the tools used to implement it, and on the human ability those tools have *thus-far* unlocked. Better tools can come - e.g. better source-control systems or collaboration systems or IDEs or something else, which can then influence a different type of methodology.

I love online evangelism and people that champion causes. But I'd advise against becoming devoted infantry-men under the banner of methods or tools. Instead, by looking at methods as transitional, in a continuous state of flux towards improvement, and bounded by the limits of current tools, we can do better innovative thinking.

As an example of this - Bret Victor's work on creating programming environments with instant feedback (see his talk INVENTING ON PRINCIPLE[1]), has greatly influenced discussion and experimentation on how to evolve code IDEs and project management methods, and even source-control, resulting in products like LIGHT TABLE[2] and FLOWHUB[3] that offer that new alternative views on the methods used to build things.

Outside of programming, this dance applies to productivity in every other industry as well. Take HR - if their current recruiting method involves written interview tests, the common HRM tools they use are fine, since they are built around that. But if the new emerging tools get better aligned with things like challenge or puzzle-based recruiting, the HR teams

---

1   "Bret Victor - Inventing on Principle", Vimeo.com, Feb 10, 2012. https://vimeo.com/36579366

2   "LightTable - The Next Generation Code Editor", Lighttable.com, Accessed Jan 4, 2016. http://lighttable.com/

3   "Flowhub - Peer-to-peer full-stack visual programming for your fingers", Flowhub, Accessed Jan 4, 2016. https://flowhub.io/

will have something they can use to adopt those modern methods of hiring.

Too often startup companies start from the question "What are customers currently doing?" and just make something for that, which results in products that are similar to every other product in the market. But understanding this Meta Pattern, a better question is "Why are they stuck doing things the current way - what part of the existing tools in the market limit them from exploring other methodologies or approaches?" and building out from there.

BONUS PATTERN (A CLASSIC): PRODUCT DIFFERENTIATION CYCLE

Products first compete on features, then on personalization, then on new "gateway" features, then on personalization...

THIS ONE I WAS introduced to in a book about a decade ago - alas I forget which one (if it was your book, please let me know so I can update this text). Since then however, I've been observing nearly all product categories going through this.

All products go through a first phase where they compete on feature-differentiation. They'll try and one-up each other by adding new and interesting things or abilities. Here, all the marketing is focused on the features / abilities / awesome new things the user can do with it.

At some point, the marginal value of adding new features for a typical customer goes below a certain threshold - essentially the new features stop incentivizing people to buy. At this point, that product cycle enters into a phase of competing only over aesthetic or design differentiation, since all products roughly have feature-parity. Here you start to have the products evolve like fashion accessories - marketing their sizes and shapes and colors and weight and trendiness, having celebrities weigh in on their awesomeness, and so on.

Once they get to this holding pattern, they stay there until some breakthrough "gateway" technology comes along which makes a step-function increase in demand based on that new feature, which starts that cycle all over again.

This is most cleanly illustrated in the evolution of mobile devices from 1999 onward. Classic (read: dumb) phones had an intense phase of differentiating on features - here's a camera phone, this one has GPS, this one has a built-in calendar, etc. Then eventually, the differentiation ran dry, as more or less all phones started getting feature parity, and an era of "phones as fashion" began. You might remember the Moto Razr from this time. Hundreds of shapes, sizes, colors, sleekness. It was madness for mobile-app developers on dumb-phones.

Eventually, the "gateway technology" of capacitive

touch-screens became just cheap enough to manufacture, that smart-phones could be built. This kicked off another cycle of feature-enhancements for a few generations (here's Siri, and Apps, and fingerprint readers, etc. etc.). Now smartphones are in a holding pattern again, competing on being the thinnest and largest and blingiest.

Throughout this cycle, marketing is able to make people feel excited about every new gen, in a way that it feels like something fresh and novel, but if you can see the underlying Meta Pattern, it's predictable and old. In fact, Apple's playbook follows this Meta Pattern to a tee. They did this with the Macs, then with iPods, then iPhones, then iPads. You can almost predict the next layers of phone differentiation cycles by looking at which manufacturing component technologies are entering into that "now feasible for mass production" price range (about $20-40 BOM change at scale). Maybe it will be flexible OLEDs in a few years.

What's less obvious, at least from when I speak about this to people, is that this cycle applies to *all* product types.

Most notably, it's heavily in play in the SAAS based software industry right now. About seven years ago, around the time Basecamp came around, there was a push from old project management software and other bulky counter-parts, to newer, lighter, better designed ones, where feature-differentiation was in play. But the past few years, the SAAS industry is stagnating with uninspired products - essentially making the same thing with the same features again and again, only differentiating on visual design. You'll see this whenever a new design method becomes hip. For example, Google's Material Design was announced in 2014, followed by, over the past year, a whole new influx of startups announcing "new products" that are exactly same thing as other startups, only now with Material Design. (I don't feel like calling out specific names here because I'm sure those startups can evolve further).

Now, there's an interesting argument I hear sometimes: "Customers just expect good design now. After the iPad, if you don't have awesomely designed apps, no one buys." But that's how I know the web software industry is in that phase. If you feel or think that way, you are literally confirming that substantive marginal value for new products in the eyes of customers are coming from design changes, and no longer from features. Which then implies that you might just be making (feature or ability-wise) whatever everyone else is making, without substantive improvements.

Which then leads to someone like me writing this book. To hopefully get you to think about radically new abilities or features to make, that can kickstart a new cycle.

You see how we're all just fish, flowing at the whim of the Meta Pattern.

The other counter-point I'd add is that you know you've hit that next breakthrough "gateway" tech precisely because people stop caring about how crummy the UI is (at least temporarily) as long as they're able to get those new super-human abilities. That's a bit where Virtual Reality or Augmented Reality are right now, and I've seen this a number of times with clients at Mocha7.

So yeah, Meta Patterns. There are literally dozens more to talk about, but best leave those for another time. Identify and understand them well, and you can start to predict the future like an analyst. Do that, and you can start to think more innovatively.

20 PICK AN IMPOSSIBLE TARGET AND GET MAD ABOUT IT

As a discipline of how to push your mind to think better, sometimes you just have to "CHOOSE TO GO TO THE MOON[1]".

Sometimes it's just good to set an impossible target, and get obsessed about nailing it. Something that is quite obviously broad, and will never really be solved per se, and might even feel silly to do, but is useful to frame our thoughts towards innovation anyway.

For example: "We're going to *fix* education - once and for all... enough is enough... let's just crack it."

---

1   "We Choose to go to the Moon", Youtube clip, Uploaded Oct 7, 2007. https://www.youtube.com/watch?v=g25G1M4EXrQ

That obsession of *solving it once and for all* frames a certain type of thinking - one where you start to feel that no other product or company in that market gets it; no one else has been able to crack this because all other solutions are awful. After all, if they weren't, nobody would be talking about how said market needs fixing, and *everyone* would be using that dominant product.

It then helps you try and figure out *why* those other solutions are awful, which helps understand customer needs that are not served well.

For the Education example, it would help figure out which parts of the education market aren't working, and how to systemize those parts into achievable targets, and then build solutions around them.

You don't actually "fix education", sure. You don't end up on the moon you were shooting for. But you do get to space. You do end up with solutions that are significantly more meaningful than through other approaches.

What's more, it gives everyone in your team a bearing on the big picture. When your company's initial solution succeeds, the impossible target gives you a direction to keep pushing towards before complacency sets. You could keep asking that question every couple of years or in every internal design jam ("how do we *fix* education - once and for all?") that'll keep creating new and interesting solutions that haven't really been done or thought of before.

Solutions made through this simple method would certainly be better than: "We help brands run surveys and polls on their Facebook pages, and that's an immense opportunity". I'm pretty sure no one is saying "Gosh darn it - lets *fix* how people connect with brands - finally".

A common followup question on this is how to find that one impossible target that really works for you. There are two very effective and simple ways.

The first I'd call the "Hilariously Broken" approach. This is inspired by SETH GODIN'S AWESOME TED TALK "THIS IS BROKEN"[2] (also, buy his books). Notice in particular, how he says "broken". It's not a statement of fact, it's a word to put all the disdain and frustration about a situation into. When there's just no other way of describing it. When you find yourself looking at something and thinking, "this is... just... broken. Hilariously broken." then you know you have an impossible target worth working on. There are lots of hilariously broken things around us: from airport check-ins; to objectivity in journalism; to healthcare; to how startups can find investors that share their beliefs; to how real, new knowledge is being ignored in the age of noisy "experts", etc.

I wrote this book because I found myself thinking that the startup ecosystem's seeming drive towards mediocre, incremental solutions was hilariously broken (there's a Comedy

---

2   "Seth Godin - This is Broken!", Gel Conference. Youtube clip. Uploaded on Jun 20, 2014. https://www.youtube.com/watch?v=nZiDS-4Xd2k

TV show about it from the creator of *Beavis and Butt-head*, it's that hilariously broken). My impossible target with that is "Get the world to think more innovatively".

The other approach comes from the 1976 movie "Network". I've had many aspiring entrepreneurs ask me what the best reason is to start a company. This is it.

It's when you are so utterly frustrated with the state of affairs of something that you feel like getting up off of your seat, opening a window, sticking your head out and yelling out that *you're as mad as hell, and you're not gonna take it anymore* over and over again. (See THE SCENE[3] for reference.) In my mind, that is the only best reason to start a company, because that obsessive drive is what will carry you through the brutally hard parts of building a company and having the courage to innovate when the entire world around you wants you to seek smaller improvements and do data-driven decisions (oops).

I had that type of "I'm as mad as hell and I'm not gonna take this anymore!" moment several years ago when it came to the productivity and work software space. And that led to the stealth work we're doing at CDF Software. And we're still pretty mad, and we still can't take it anymore.

Pick an impossible target, and get mad about it. The rest will sort itself out.

---

3   "Network - Mad as Hell Scene", Youtube Clip, Uploaded on Feb 24, 2008. https://www.youtube.com/watch?v=WINDtlPXmmE

21 TO INNOVATE, STOP LISTENING TO BOZOS LIKE ME

I LOVE GUY KAWASAKI'S TALK on THE ART OF THE START[1]. It's worth a listen every few months to stay grounded (P.S. buy his book).

One term Guy uses is also relevant to innovation-thinking. Sometimes, to innovate, you just have to ignore the people who think they know what you should do - the "bozos". Like me. And this book.

As an entrepreneur, one thing you'll need to tell yourself from time to time is you are ultimately the one to make the decisions on how to move your own company and products

---

1   "Guy Kawasaki 'The Art of the Start' @ TiECon 2006", Youtube clip, Uploaded May 1, 2011. https://www.youtube.com/watch?v=jSlwuafyUUo

forward.

Everyone will jump at the chance to give you ~~opinions~~ advice (or wax poetic about their love-affair with coffee), but no one else will have seen the very specific situation or context that you're facing in the moment of that decision. No one else will understand the exact problems you're solving; the dynamics of that industry of customers; the exact team you're going to war with; the exact connections and relationships you have; the exact amount of goodwill or allies you've garnered around you.

It's easy for people to say "well why don't you just hire rockstars and the code will sort itself out?" or "it's not the ideas that matter, but the execution" or "dude just predict the future based on this Meta Pattern like fishes in the river" or something.

It's hard to commit the money, time and energy to get it done. Only you can ultimately have the complete picture in mind to be able to make that decision. You'll have to be the one that actually spends that money, hoping for that strategy payoff and that return.

So consider your unique and specific understanding of your situation an asset and advantage for you - maybe that insight alone will give you clever or innovative ways forward.

Good luck. All I can tell you is: I believe in you. And when you make it to the other side, let me know you made it so we can have some deep, deep coffee together.

And if you find things hard and desperate and no one to talk to, remember I believe in you. Let me know, so we can talk.

Until then, ignore me, ignore this book, ignore lean methods (please?), build a lens through which to see the world and get innovating.

22 CONCLUSIONS: SO WHAT'S REALLY THE MATTER WITH LEAN METHODS?

WELL, NOTHING REALLY.

(Sorry if you were expecting a David vs Goliath type of faceoff.)

Lean methods, incremental improvements, "improve on the competition", data-confirmed and focus-tested hypothesis creation etc - they are honestly sometimes the best approach to take, depending on what your situation is. Infact, just after writing the first draft of this book, I met three entrepreneurs who - for one reason or another - could really benefit from looking into lean methods.

It could be the team is operating in a domain they are inexperienced in. In that case, it is best to take it very slow to build up the key relationships and understand a repeatable formula for sales before scaling (although, my advice is to never start a company in a domain you haven't built some deep understanding of the dynamics of).

It could be the idea or solution is just so weird that there's no good framework to get a sense of whether or not it could work (weird is good though). So the best thing is just to say: "Well, let's just try it out and see what happens - but let's just start with a very small outlay". An example of this could be VINE - I don't think I could have determined it to be as successful as it is, because it depended on the community figuring out how to create "fun" out of a strange video format that no one had played with before.

Sometimes the solution is controversial, but not in a "polarizing the market" way but more in the *"this can either bring world peace or cause world war III"* way. Maybe the solution is relating to an area of high cultural sensitivity or something where the culture of the customers isn't really understood so we don't know if a particular marketing message would be good or offensive. For that, even the dreaded scourge of the startup world - focus-testing - could work, or improving on existing solutions, or a super-quiet soft-launch.

There are people who, for one reason or another, just don't want to build innovative solutions that can have a big impact and change the lives of customers in a big way. They just want to have a lifestyle business that pays the bills, not really wanting investors or acquisitions or large exits or big impact. For them the lean startup model would be great.

And the general essence of the lean startup approach - to continuously just try things and quickly discard things that just aren't working - is still useful for companies after they launch their first solution, to build out a continuous improvement cycle. It's useful for large enterprises to be more experimental.

I just argue that incremental improvement and experiments-driven outlay isn't the best approach for innovation, or inventive thinking, a key ingredient of entrepreneurship. It's not a good method to find that 10x "curve-jumping" improvement that builds the energy it takes to push through the inertia of change.

And I just propose that you should consider lean methods only one of the many options available to you (the LHO if you will - *just kidding!*), and only select it if that method really fits the type of business you're doing, since many useful companies or businesses need strong innovation to break through and won't fit that model well.

And hopefully I've been able to show that there are valid alternatives for thinking innovatively that are worth pursuing. With innovation-thinking orientation, you can quite often find solutions that would take about the same amount of effort to build as incremental methods, but yield much higher, more compelling, competitive or disruptive results.

In fact, in my experience the "innovative" solution often takes much less effort to build, because you've outsourced parts of the old model, or have distilled flows down to their core essence, and you're not trying to merely catch up to the market.

So in my ideal world, the one from my impossible target, entrepreneurs and teams wouldn't merely want to be safe in the incremental complacency of the status quo, watching the world pass them by. They would be innovation-thinkers.

For me, the ideal would be startups now start pitching their companies in a format something like this:

- They start with highlighting their impossible target and their un-subdued passion / madness about it.

- They explain their business in that renewed pitch format talking about how they change the economics of said in-dustry.

- They explain how they involve communities to outsource parts of their business to drastically reduce operational costs.

- They explain their team's execution techniques are all things that they figured out using the one-sentence meth-od, hence those are things the competition isn't doing.

- And they frame market trends, not just based on current data, but also on upcoming shifts coming from Meta Patterns, and how their company is ready for them.

Wouldn't that just be incredible? Or crazy. Sometimes the line is blurry between those two. Maybe coffee will help with that.

I'd certainly consider investing in a company like that, or risk being on the wrong side of history. Because that company is the dark knight, it is brazen about changing things, forever, with or without the consent of their industry*. The power always lies with founders and founding teams - if that's the type of companies they start to want to build, everyone else is going to have to get on board or be left on the station. (* um - add some legal addendum about regulated industries and the Hippocratic oath, and generally being the dark knight in lawful ways).

But if you've just been asking "who the @#$@ are you Osama A., and why should I listen to you?" You know, I don't know. Ultimately, no amount of a person's history can quite prepare him for the uncertainty of the changes ahead. I'm just someone who has trained himself to push his mind to stay open and keep thinking, and to keep listening and learning from anyone who offers a new perspective. I'm just an observer of the world around me (and subsequently, an occasional shaker of head).

And I'm someone who's always found that only through focusing on giving (rather than taking) do I find the most returns and benefit come back in whatever I'm doing.

And I've found that something I like doing immensely, is solving some of the big problems in the world, by igniting possibility in the minds of others.

So if I'm walking past a dam and there's a hole in it and water is pouring out - if I can see that the problem exists - I try and help. If I have a viewpoint of the world that may help someone else, I try to offer it.

What that's worth to you is up to you. I won't try to tell you what others have valued my time at.

So, if you're on board, let's move away from slow and steady, uncertain-until-verified, incremental, piece-by-piece improvement, chasing a shrinking percentage of existing demand. Let's aim to do things meaningful enough that they're worth paying attention to, because "companies worth paying attention to" is historically the only one-sentence essence of the companies that see massive growth.

Let's get innovating.

Oh, and if you're *very* on-board with this, help me get the message out, and get others to also start innovation-thinking. Help me reach my impossible target with this book: to get the world to think more innovatively. You and I, together, can reach that moon.

23 NEXT STEPS

THANKS FOR READING! LET me know if this book helps you in any way, it will make my day.

(Psst. There's 16 pages of addendums ahead with more on what innovation-thinking companies look like, so keep reading.)

I think there are many innovation-thinking methods still to be discovered, and it'll take all of our experiences together to find them. I'd love to learn about any you've discovered or use that have helped you in the past.

Come join the community at innovationthinking.org/nextsteps and let's find more.

If you really like innovation-thinking, and you'd like to work in a place that applies it daily, then join us at CDF Software. We're applying these methods to solve really interesting and hard problems, like how to make people more productive at work. We'd love to hear about you at work@cdfsoftware. com.

Mocha7's team does consulting on innovation, product and marketing strategy. You can email them at hello@mocha7. com. (I sometimes consult through them for enterprise clients or governments).

You can also find me at @CoffeeAndOsama - I have a few other books I'm thinking of so we can talk about them there.

And if you're a startup, I'm always open to mentoring or advisory things if you're up to having a bozo in your life.

See you in some coffee shop out there.

NOTES
AND
ADDENDUMS

NOTES

ON COMPETITION

The book mentioned the notions of creating new markets or going into a market where there's no competition. But that's in an abstract sense of positioning yourself differently to existing competitors. In reality the competitors are still competitors and remain, and you shouldn't really carry yourself (esp in investor meetings) as if competitors don't exist. Also, whatever new market you create won't last very long - think weeks or so. It's faster for people to copy you and try and catch a piece than ever before.

ON STEALTH MODE FOR STARTUPS

In general, you shouldn't do stealth mode if you can avoid it. There's two wrong reasons to do stealth: To build hype, or to sit in a cave and wait until you have a good product. But there are other reasons for stealth. You can find customers, get feedback from customers and do trials and evaluations with customers while in stealth, you are just making the product not available for general consumption yet. The debate comes down to: do you need a statistically sizable sampling of feedback (through general availability) or a very select, chosen set of feedback that's from the people that are your best representatives of the target use-case (stealth). Another reason for stealth is you've already gone out and gathered a lot of feedback and there are tonnes of things to fix before the next round of feedback, and in between so you need to just focus - this is the limited alpha / beta approach.

COMPETING WITH OTHER STARTUPS

Startups shouldn't be obsessed about competing with other startups, especially when there's an incumbent to beat. There's sometimes a fine line between competitor and partner, and sometimes it makes more sense to build a strong alliance against the larger foe. A small example: I've seen a case where two companies each with two founders were struggling to do the same type of company, but got going more easily with them agreeing to become one company with four people.

INNOVATION AND THE LEAN STARTUP METHODS ARE COMPATIBLE TOO

Innovation-thinking helps mainly in two areas - (1) conception / vision phase of what the company / product should be. (2) Day to day techniques and methods used to execute (marketing, UX design etc). In between these two is a gap where it's still fine to use lean-startup methods. The gap is "ok, so how do we actually start? What's our version 1? When do we come to market?"

But even there, the lean-startup model isn't the only way of addressing that gap. Sometimes the product needs a big push out the door at launch, so must have a compelling story that surprises and inspires customers, so an MVP and soft-launch and assumption testing wouldn't work (conversely, the lean startup model is happy to say that sometimes an MVP is a huge project taking 5 years to make - maybe a factory or something... that's the minimum to test viability.)

TECHNOLOGY ALONE ISN'T AN INNOVATION-THINKING METHOD

You'll notice I didn't say "Technological breakthroughs" as an innovation-thinking method. I'm an engineer at heart, and still involved in technical matters. But in my experience, focusing on cool tech first, very rarely also creates compelling stories about market shifts. Most of the startup companies I've seen fail have been the ones who went too deep on a cool tech library or hook they built and spent all their time desperately trying to find market-fit with some sort of solution for it, until they ran out of energy. I've always advocated that "Technology is just a catalyst to use to get to the product you've already thought of" and it works best when the product and business is first designed independently, and then we look at what type of technology will need to be built to get us there. Or e.g. in product management, you would describe the solution first as the ideal story, and then figure out if it can actually be built.

ONE THING I LEARNED WRITING THIS: IS IT EVER HARD TO WRITE THE OPENING OF A NON-FICTION BOOK

I had heard from authors before that the opening of the book takes the most time. It took almost twice as long to write the front matter of this book than the actual methods. I did about 41 rewrites of the opening chapter, sometimes becoming 20+ pages. So, that's something I learned the hard way then - it is *really* hard to figure out book starts.

ADDENDUM: THE CRISIS OF OBSCURITY AND THE INNOVATION IMPERATIVE

This is one risk in the market that I think more people should be worried about. I talked about this in the opening chapter in a short paragraph, but here I'll try and explain it more using an abstract model. The model itself is broad and general (and thus doesn't apply to all cases), but gets a point across.

So, I think of creating anything - products, books, etc - as overcoming the inertia to change. Inertia of convincing yourself to do it, convincing others to join you, convincing customers, convincing investors, etc.

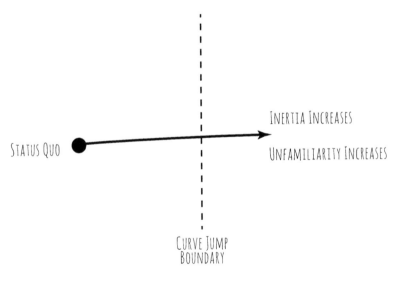

FIG 1. THE INERTIA MODEL

Overcoming inertia to change is the heart of substantial innovation. The more forward-thinking, ambitious, and world-changing thing you want to do, the farther you have to go from the status quo, and thus the more inertia you'd have to overcome.

Imagine it looking something like Fig 1 on previous page.

Think of the status-quo as a dot in the center, and as you move away from it, the inertia keeps increasing, and so does the unfamiliarity of the customer with the solution. Far enough away from this status-quo is a "curve jump" boundary, something that moves the industry in newer directions (e.g. smartphones vs dumb phones).

Now you can think of it as: the further you want to move the users away into the unfamiliar, the more amazing the solution needs to be, to overcome that larger amount of inertia, cynicism, doubt.

On the other hand, if you only want to overcome a small amount of inertia, you would need a smaller amount of effort and less substantial change, and less overall energy to handle it.

Side Note: These are only broadly true as an abstract model. There are ofcourse exceptions, of innovative things that are still familiar. But generally the "crazier" the idea the more unfamiliar it might be compared to the status quo.

Let's think about how lean methods fall into this model. Lean methods tend to focus on a few things, like: (1) Minimize outlay required to revenue (2) Focus almost exclusively on Customer Discovery for product development (as opposed to Problem Discovery or Solution Discovery), and (3) Minimize the risks in total for the startup to fail.

So they could fit the model somewhat like Figure 2 below.

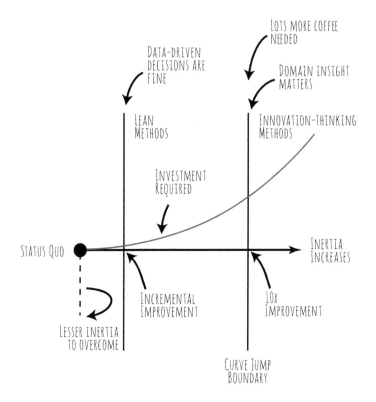

FIG 2. INCREMENTAL VS 10X

To minimize the risk, you try not to offer something unfamiliar. Just enough "different" that a customer will pay, but not something that would require greater sales effort, or training, or increase the risk of customer not getting it, in case that slows down the sales process. So you might stay closer to the status-quo, and might look only at existing demand, so customers already understand how to evaluate something, and need minimal understanding or evaluation to get on-board.

The solutions wouldn't really need detailed domain knowledge. The problems are generally easily understood, and can be gathered by just looking at competitors, or looking at user behavior in data, or by directly asking customers what they want. Data-driven decisions are fine.

On the other hand, the curve-jump solutions on the right, are the ones that may require innovation-thinking.

The things made by innovation-thinking are hard enough to crack sometimes that they require solutions that cover everything strategically - from product, to marketing, to organizational planning. They innovate on everything - production; distribution; business and pricing models, community management, etc.

They might require more investment (Again, lots of exceptions) - they're creating a new market, so may need more communication, more training, longer sales cycles, longer R&D and product development or QA cycles, etc.

They require specialized domain insights and knowledge about the problems being solved - to reveal the things beyond what the data might be showing, or even beyond what customers may be saying they want. Most often, here, even the problems aren't well defined. It takes a different type of organizational model, a different workflow for pacing out R&D, problem discovery, solution discovery, etc.

These companies do "Design-thinking" and "Innovation-thinking" in tandem. They are more obsessed with getting a thousand details just right.

And it takes a particular type of support structure around them, one that understands what curve-jumps need.

Still, both of these can co-exist in the market and be fine initially. That's until the problem happens (it's happening now).

THE PROBLEM OF OBSCURITY

Lean methods require less investment, and present less risk, and have a higher chance for customers to buy sooner, starting revenue sooner. That creates a strong economic incentive for more investors, mentors and advisors to try and encourage that.

The problem is what that incentive does.

More startups are doing that - *lots more*. And all of them are just incrementally improving on one another, just adding small things here and there to get the sale but keep it highly familiar.

That creates what I'd simply call an "abundance of same-y products". Too many of the same types of products start to litter the market.

Attention economics kicks in - customers start to pay less and less attention to each of those products. See Figure 3.

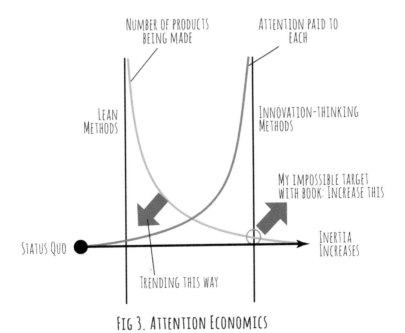

FIG 3. ATTENTION ECONOMICS

I'm seeing this already in action in terms of declining ROI on all marketing / PR efforts for all types of marketing (Content Marketing, SEO, SEM, social marketing, community building etc) for incremental products in crowded spaces. (i.e. you have to now invest more and more for comparable returns)

The problem is, as more and more startups are getting added on the "small improvement" side, its pushing that curve downwards.

Attention is flattening sharply, approaching zero.

So in an age of abundance of same-y products, doing incremental improvements greatly increases the risk of obscurity for startups, and ironically in turn greatly increases their risk of failure.

It is far worse for a startup to be obscure - for no one to know it or care about it - than for it to run out of money. If you run out of money but have a devoted, loving user-base, there are options. (see Evernote's history, or public classical radio).

From the data that I'm seeing, the age of abundance has come, and a startup going into crowded product spaces using incremental improvement may greatly increase risk of failure. The companies with the same products, or the same techniques, done for the same stuff from the same startup advice... it isn't working.

Attention is only going to get worse. You're going to just have to absolutely nail it out of the park, or its just not going to get noticed.

But here's the opportunity: On the "curve-jump" side, attention increases substantially, while there are fewer companies doing anything there. So investing in the curve-jump side actually becomes a larger opportunity.

Another interesting bit from this abstract model - the more you're investing, in more substantial products, the more attention customers may give.

BUT WHAT ABOUT THIS LARGER INITIAL INVESTMENT? I'M JUST A STARTUP

So yeah, on the face of it curve-jumps need a larger initial investment.

But here's where innovation-thinking kicks in.

Innovation-thinking can help you rethink every business function, helping to rapidly reduce the cost it takes to do substantial things. It is that classic startup conundrum where innovation thrives: We only have this much money, and have to get that much attention, how do we figure this out? Many startups do.

So, with continuous innovation-thinking and scrappiness at each decision or stage, while the overall initial investment may still be higher because of more investment in education / training of customers, it can still be within the same effort / money range as the typical startup can afford to do (Unless you really are just starting with nothing and hoping to bootstrap).

The bottom line though, is the next decade is marred by an Innovation Imperative: you must do 10x or just risk dying. You must create unfamiliar, unique, different things that will be harder to explain to customers but more valuable to them, or you risk dying.

Then again, maybe I'm just over-caffeinated.

ADDENDUM: THE INNOVATION-THINKING COMPANY

I've been thinking for some time what a company that says "we're an innovation-thinking" company looks like. CDF is certainly that company, and it has been educational to see how applying innovation-thinking has evolved our internal workflows.

Adding innovation-thinking as a key part of day-to-day life affects many other things that a company does.

This company would apply innovation-thinking not just in their product but in every facet of their company - in pricing models, in how they do customer support, how they do distribution, how they think about handling PR situations, how they think about inventory or warehousing or branding or HR management or fundraising (with limits - we don't want too much creativity in finance and accounting and regulated matters).

There are many specific questions and models and unsolved problems about day-to-day operations that result from that, but it comes down to being a company that is about a few fundamental things.

It comes to being a company that focuses on doing substantial things worth noticing as a driver of growth. Most of its conversations of growth come from doing the things that other products are simply not trying.

It comes to being an internal team that is comfortable with, and often primarily driven by, exploring things that are still largely unknown. That takes a certain type of team - one that stays on-course if it comes across a large unknown problem along the way to progress, one where it may not even know all the smaller problems it'll have to solve first to figure out how to solve the bigger unknown. (Picture this like the teams that ask "Why don't we make self-driving cars?" or "Why don't we put a private rocket in space?" - those are large unknowns).

It comes to being a company and having a board that is long-term focused, and is patient about making many attempts to reach substantial improvements, and being comfortable about learning from failures along the way.

And it comes to being a company that leads with new insights and new techniques on most every operational function.

I've been wondering if this company will be misunderstood, since its vocabulary wouldn't always match others. Will it always have a harder time trying to convince people that their newer models are good despite being unfamiliar, or will it find support because they are out-of-the-box thinkers.

I think the answer is that there is a subset of the entrepreneurship community out there - of mentors, investors, advisors, entrepreneurs - that specifically "get" and want to support innovation-thinking as a fundamental tenant to creating companies. I've met several such individuals who hold those beliefs and encourage them in others.

But that community isn't evident or easy to find yet, particularly because startup communities tend to be one-for-all-types approaches. So there are cases of mismatch - some innovation-thinking entrepreneur trying to connect with a lean-methods believing advisor or investor. Or two innovation-thinking people in a crowd of 50 who could be great supporters of one another but they just happen to miss each other.

Maybe there should be a better way of identifying these types of companies, so it's easier for the right people to connect with them.

Maybe it starts with all of us just getting up to be recognized, by announcing that we believe in adopting and supporting innovation-thinking. That could be enough to get going in helping one another find people who could be friction-less sources of insight in our lives, and can continue to teach and discuss interesting approaches with each other.

ADDENDUM: ONE SENTENCE SUMMARIES OF THIS BOOK

One of the readers of an early draft of this book suggested using the one-sentence method on the methods themselves, to make them easier to remember. Great idea! So here's everything again as one-sentence summaries.

BE HUMAN	Don't just look for solutions from within the vocabulary of business - but seek ideas and solutions from culture, nature and humanity
FIRST PRINCIPLES THINKING	Find the most basic form of "thing", then build up from there
CHANGED STARTUP PITCH FORMULA	Cost economies in ___ market are ___, but with these key technologies, the economies can be brought down so that ____ then becomes feasible
ONE SENTENCE APPROACH	Summarize a profession / vision / product down to a single core sentence, in order to reinterpret it
FUTURE HISTORY APPROACH	In the future - 60-80 years from now, what would a historian of that time look back at as the one big thing that changed everything?
FUNDAMENTAL ASSUMPTION APPROACH	What one assumption does everyone make when making a product like this, and let's change that

BACK TO THE CUSTOMER	What part of the operations model of this type of business can you outsource back to customers? (through community participation or the product)
TAFAKKAR	Observe the smallest of details in the environment, then try to find the underlying systems in place behind that model, then find the systems in place behind those things, etc.
CONTEXT FOR LAST CHANGE	What is the context that brought about the way things work in the present in this industry - has that context changed now?
WHAT IF HISTORY NEVER HAPPENED	What if you're making the first product of this type, and no other reference exists? Considering how people live today, what should the design be?
ORIGINAL INTENT THINKING	People aren't trying to do what they're doing today - what are they originally intending to do, for which the present is the current best option?
LEAST HAPPY OPTION	Whatever best product exists in the market is the customer's Least Happy Option - how do we make a happier option?
FORCE THE INNOVATOR'S DILEMMA	How do you position the product that competitors cannot offer that without having to kill their own product line or marketing message
ASSUME YOUR CUSTOMERS ALREADY HAVE THE COMPETITOR'S PRODUCT	Stop thinking too much about competitors by assuming the customer already has their product. Then you're free to think about what to make that still makes a customer switch over.

LOOK AT THE NEGATIVE SPACE OF POSSIBILITY	The negative space has a better question. Not how many are there already, but why isn't everyone else there?
REINTERPRET FOUNDING VISION	The founding vision of a company is the purest and least affected by reality - it helps to reinterpret it over time for changing circumstances, but to remain close to it
EDGES OF YOUR INDUSTRY	It's helpful to not get so engrained in the culture and day-to-day of an industry to lose objectivity on how things can be better, and useful to take inspiration from other industries.
META PATTERNS	Patterns of patterns of change. (1) What's premium today becomes commoditized tomorrow, leading to a new premium. (2) Productivity industry dances between tools and techniques, (3) Products first differentiate on features, then on design, then on new gateway features, then design... many more.
IMPOSSIBLE TARGETS	Align your company on impossible targets to fix broken things that might take a decade or more to achieve - and get as mad as hell about them.
DON'T LISTEN TO BOZOS	Ultimately, you understand the full context of your situation the best - be careful of advice from people who don't understand the domain and context that well.

#InnovationThinking

Acknowledgements

As I'm sure other authors can relate, the process of putting ones framework of thought into a book to be published can be very stressful and full of inertia. So I'm thankful to everyone who's helped me throughout the process.

I want to thank my wife Amna for being a source of positive energy throughout the exercise of writing the book. She was always quick to drop whatever she was doing to review and edit the latest draft, provide immensely useful suggestions and ideas, and give feedback on all the details that led to final polish. Most importantly though, I'm thankful for her continuous encouragement throughout the process.

Thanks to all the people who took time out to review an early draft of this book and offered feedback as well as positive early commentary.

Thanks to eveyrone at Next Thirty Press and Mocha7, in particular Anita Santa-Coloma, for help with putting this book out into the world.

Everyone at CDF Software and Mocha7, past and present, for working hard and pushing one another towards more innovative thinking daily, and building the culture through which these methods were realized. In particular, Qazi Atiq and Justen Andrews.

Thanks to everyone who kept checking in and asking me when I'd get back to writing on innovation. And thanks to the Green & White community, and all the participants and organizers of Startup Insiders, for some great coffee sessions together.

ABOUT THE AUTHOR

Osama A. Hashmi is a U.K. citizen and currently lives in Seattle, WA.

He is the CEO and Product Architect of CDF Software - a productivity innovation company he founded. He is also the President of the Innovation and Product Strategy consulting firm Mocha7, a company he co-founded.

He has been attributed to instigating an active entrepreneurship culture in Pakistan and South Asia. To build a startup ecosystem in Asia, he founded a tech community and publication Green & White (100,000 strong - publication later acquired), and was also the Principal and Co-Founder of an entrepreneurship support program called Startup Insiders (2,000 members; 400+ companies; 150 mentors). Startup Insiders was influential in kick-starting a startup community that now boasts several accelerators, incubators and funds in the region).

He has advised government policy-makers on entrepreneurship and startup investment policy, and through Mocha7 has helped government-backed startup programs in France, Spain, South Korea and elsewhere.

Prior to CDF Software, he was the founder of a telecom hardware startup building a smartphone device (prior to the iPhone), and was working as a Management Consultant and Analyst on Product Strategy and Operations design. Prior to that he was involved as a technical lead for Enterprise Software Solutions for Supply Chain and Operations Management, PLM and BPR.

He has advised Fortune 500 companies, board-level decision makers at consumer tech companies as well as startups on product and competitiveness strategy, and has overseen more than 300 product launches. He has also informally mentored over 90 startup companies.

In the past, he has written extensively about innovation, entrepreneurship and product strategy and has been a panelist at various conferences, such as the Innovation in Journalism conference at Stanford.

He graduated with B.Sc. Computer Engineering from The University of Texas at Austin, and was trained further on Advanced Enterprise Solutions Architecture and Intelligent Supply Chain Management in his early career.

His response to the question: "Would you like some coffee?" is typically "Wait, how is that even a question?"

He likes Cello and Erhu music, science-fiction, and stargazing.

A NOTE FROM NEXT THIRTY PRESS

Thank you for reading this book, from everyone here at Next Thirty Press.

This book is for people going through startup incubators and accelerators, for startup teams and innovation focused teams in larger companies or non-profits.

Special quantity sales with discounts and special orders with custom covers can be made with us in case you are considering bringing this book to your organization.

Please email specialrequests@next30.press and we will be happy to see what we can do for you.

NEXT THIRTY PRESS

CPSIA information can be obtained
at www.ICGtesting.com
Printed in the USA
LVOW06s0923250617
539308LV00024B/116/P